Korean Home Cooking

Quick, easy, delicious recipes to make at home

The Essential Asian Kitchen

Korean Home Cooking

SOON YOUNG CHUNG

PERIPLUS

First published in the United States in 2002 by Periplus Editions (HK) Ltd., with editorial offices at 153 Milk Street, Boston, Massachusetts 02109 and 130 Joo Seng Road #06-01/03 Olivine Building Singapore 368357

© Copyright 2002 Lansdowne Publishing Pty Ltd

Library of Congress Cataloging-in-Publication Data is available.
ISBN 0-7946-5006-6

DISTRIBUTED BY

North America
Tuttle Publishing
Distribution Center
Airport Industrial Park
364 Innovation Drive
North Clarendon, VT 05759-9436
Tel: (802) 773-8930
Tel: (800) 526-2778

Japan and Korea
Tuttle Publishing
RK Building, 2nd Floor
2-13-10 Shimo-Meguro,
Meguro-Ku
Tokyo 153 0064
Tel: (03) 5437-0171
Fax: (03) 5437-0755

Asia Pacific
Berkeley Books Pte. Ltd.
130 Joo Seng Road
#06-01/03
Olivine Building
Singapore 368357
Tel: (65) 280-3320
Fax: (65) 280-6290

The publishers would like to thank Mi Hang Joo, Maeve O'Meara and Angus Cameron for their contribution to this book.

Commissioned by Deborah Nixon
Recipes: Soon Young Chung
Translation: Mi Hang Joo
Recipe Development: Angus Cameron
Introduction: Maeve O'Meara
Language Consultant: Dr Duk-Soo Park
Photographer: Louise Lister
Stylist: Suzie Smith
Designer: Robyn Latimer
Editor: Merry Morgan Pearson
Production Manager: Sally Stokes
Project Coordinator: Alexandra Nahlous

First Edition
06 05 04 03 02   10 9 8 7 6 5 4 3 2 1

Set in Spartan Classified on QuarkXPress
Printed in Singapore

A note on the romanization of Korean words
The Korean government made changes to the romanization of Korean words in 2000. This book uses the revised romanization system. However, as kimchi is well known and has become part of the English language usage, the romanization remains as kimchi not "gimchi."

Cover image: Japchae, page 48
Page 1: Stuffed cucumber (Oi sobaegi), page 26
Page 2: Kimchi and tofu (Kimchi dubu), page 66
Page 3: Fresh vegetable bibimbap (Sanchae bibimbap), page 40
Opposite: Octopus kabobs (Nakji sanjeok), page 81

Contents

Introduction 8
The art of Korean cooking • Kimchi • Geography and produce • Historical development • Food preparation • How to prepare and serve dinner • Etiquette • Festivals • Drinks

Equipment 16

Ingredients 17

Kimchi 22
Watery radish kimchi
Chinese cabbage kimchi
Stuffed cucumber
White Chinese cabbage kimchi

Appetizers 31
Korean mung bean pancakes
Green lentil jelly
Jellyfish with vegetables

Gujeolpan
Pine nut porridge
Mung bean porridge
Soybean porridge
Abalone porridge
Red bean porridge

Noodles and rice 40
Fresh vegetable bibimbap
Bibimbap
Hot noodles
Bibimmyeon
Cold noodles
Japchae
Fried octopus with chili pepper sauce and noodles

Soups 52
Dumpling soup
Ginseng chicken soup
Beef ball soup
Seaweed soup
Dumpling and rice cake soup

Vegetables 58
Stuffed zucchini
Three-color vegetables
Stuffed mushrooms with beef
Kimchi and tofu
Seaweed salad
Beef and bamboo shoots
Tofu and vegetable soup

Seafood 72
Mussels with soy dressing
Mussel kabobs
Squid kabobs
Squid bulgogi
Squid with sour red chili paste sauce
Steamed dried pollack fish
Octopus kabobs
Steamed shrimp with pine nut sauce
Grilled fish
Mixed seafood casserole

Chicken 89
Seasoned whole chicken
Sweet chicken wings
Fried chicken breast
Grilled chicken drumsticks
Chicken kabobs

Beef and pork 96
Fried pork with green onions
Barbecued beef
Grilled pork
Boiled Beef
Beef kabobs
Beef with pine nut sauce
Salt bulgogi
Steamed beef spare ribs
Seobsanjeok
Seobsanjeok kabobs

Desserts 113
Honey dates
Sticky rice pancakes
Rice and malt drink
Berry punch
Nashi pear dessert
Cinnamon cookies
Cinnamon fruit punch with dried persimmon

Sauces and pastes 120
Soybean paste
Hot red chili paste
Beef marinade

Glossary 122

Index 124

Guide to weights and measures 128

Introduction

I have always had a particular fascination and interest in cooking. As a young girl growing up in Korea, I was always helping my mother with one meal preparation or another, so I learned very early the many ways to enjoy nature's gifts. In this book I have included many Korean favorites, to give you a taste of authentic cooking. These include:

Bulgogi, which is barbecued beef, is one of the most famous dishes outside Korea, after kimchi. It is cooked at the table on a specially designed griddle and served wrapped in lettuce leaves with vegetables and various condiments.

Bibimbap, which is a very popular dish in Korea, changes from region to region. The basic recipe starts with a layer of rice in a very hot stone bowl. The rice is topped with seasoned stir-fried vegetables, such as mushrooms, zucchini, bean sprouts, dried kelp and green onions, and strips of beef cooked with soy sauce, sesame oil and garlic. Red bean paste and a whole raw egg are placed on top to make a sauce that is cooked by the heat of the stone bowl. It is delicious.

Naengmyeon, which is cold buckwheat noodles, is made with buckwheat noodles served cold in a chilled beef broth finished with a dash of hot mustard and the finest slivers of pear, nashi pear or apple, finely cut cucumber and half a hard-boiled egg. The noodles are chewy and very refreshing in summer. This is a real delicacy.

Japchae, which is a lovely mix of slivers of vegetables such as carrot and green onion with slivers of marinated meat and bean thread noodles, is finished with a dash of soy sauce, sesame oil and toasted sesame seeds. It is very popular at holiday dinners and birthday parties.

Gujeolpan, which is served in a nine-section dish, contains mini wheat pancakes in the center section, surrounded by slivers of beef, mushrooms, bean sprouts, finely shredded egg and slivers of vegetables. This elegant starter is eaten by rolling three or four of the fillings with a touch of soy sauce or mustard in a pancake.

Haemul jeon-gol, which is a seafood hotpot ("jeon-gol" actually means stew or casserole), is made with assorted seafood, including scallops, clams in their shells, squid, octopus or even crabs or lobsters cooked with ground red chili and vegetables.

The art of Korean cooking

Korean food is defined by its beautifully presented, fresh-tasting ingredients and healthy diet of greens, seafood, lean meats, and savory seasonings. It is a celebration of culture and tradition—much of what is eaten in Korea today is the same as was eaten centuries ago, and the preparation of food is a link with the past and with ancestors. This has ensured the continuity of Korea's unique culture, religion and language, and the traditional provincial way of life is as strong as ever, even in the high-tech, high-rise cities.

The essence of Korean cuisine is the harmony of the five tastes—hot, bitter, sweet, sour and salty—and spices are used for health and nutrition as much as for their taste. Well-seasoned, spicy vegetables, grains and seafood give Korean food its distinctive flavor.

The most distinctive Korean food is kimchi—fermented cabbage, radish, green onions, and cucumber, often spiced with red chili powder and garlic. A meal without kimchi is unthinkable—it would be seen as incomplete, lacking in style and grace. Along with soy sauce, soybean paste, sesame oil and red chili pepper paste, kimchi is one of the most important tastes of Korea.

The use of seasonings, or "yangnyeom," is seen to be very healthy, a notion that has its origins in Chinese practice. The word "yangnyeom" comes from the Chinese word for remedy, and the many plants and herbs used to prepare daily meals are also used in Chinese herbal medicines.

Traditional Korean food was labor intensive, and women were the cooks. In most meals meat or fish and rice were served with at least five different side dishes. Now, however, some of the more elaborate dishes are scaled down, and some side dishes are available in shops.

Koreans love to share meals, and eating out is commonplace. Fast-food chains abound. Korea's answer to fast family restaurants—a chain called Our Story—offers a modern spin on Korean food. It serves a Caesar-style salad with strips of fried chicken marinated in honey, soy sauce and molasses plus radish and cucumber and chestnuts rolled in bacon on a bed of iceberg lettuce. The other big seller on the menu is spicy chili beef ribs—a version on Korea's popular charcoal braised rib dish, "galbi."

The focus in Korea is on health, so it is one of the world's top markets for products such as ginseng, which is grown throughout the country.

Most open markets have special ginseng stalls where ginseng root, milk and honey are pureed in a blender for a fast health drink. The Korean diet, with its emphasis on lean grilled meats, many vegetables and steamed rice, is a very low-fat, nutritious cuisine. Add to that the health benefits from the fermentation of kimchi, which is believed to be useful in prevent cancer and maintaining a healthy bowel, and it's a great recipe for health and wellbeing.

Kimchi

Kimchi is more recently known as "gimchi," due to changes in the romanization of Korean words, and sometimes as "kimchee."

Kimchi is a traditional vegetable dish made by fermenting various kinds of vegetables, the main ones being Chinese (napa) cabbage and Japanese daikon, though there are at least a hundred different types. The vegetables are sprinkled with salt and left aside for a number of hours. They are then rinsed and seasoned with garlic, ginger, fermented fish sauce and chili powder. The vegetables are then set aside in terracotta jars to ferment—some kimchis can be used almost immediately, while others are stored for a whole winter.

Kimchi is almost a meal in itself, and the combination of rice and kimchi is the basis for breakfast, lunch and dinner. It is low in calories and cholesterol, very high in fiber and richer in vitamins than apples. Many Koreans speak of the longing and emptiness they feel if they are without kimchi for more than a day. Its hot and spicy taste stimulates the appetite, and it is full of vitamins, minerals and lactic acid.

Kimchi is so revered in Korean society that there is a large plush museum dedicated to its evolution and nutritional aspects in downtown Seoul. A timeline at the museum traces the trade over the centuries which brought new ingredients such as chili peppers, potatoes and cucumbers to the country. It also shows how kimchi looked in the third century (cured with salt) and the classic rich red look it took on once chili peppers were introduced in the seventeenth century. Reports on scientific studies about kimchi's health benefits are available and there are tastings of the many different types.

Kimchi is so essential that many rituals have developed in its preparation. At the end of the growing season, extended families, particularly in rural areas, gather to slice and cure vegetables for kimchi. This ritual, meaning the preparation of kimchi is called "gimjang." It is very important, partly because it is a means of sharing the work, but also because it passes the centuries-long traditions to the young. Seasoning requires elaborate skill and devotion.

Kimchi was traditionally stored in the ground in large ceramic jars to keep it at a stable temperature. Nowadays many families invest in a special kimchi refrigerator that is about the size of a bar refrigerator and stores a whole winter's supply at a steady 39°F (4°C).

Geography and produce

Korea is self-contained in many ways. It is bounded by water on three sides and has three powerful neighbors in China, Russia, and Japan. Although Korea was invaded by other countries at various times during the last one thousand years, its culture and food have remained distinct and separate.

Koreans are one ethnic family and speak one language. They are believed to be the descendants of several Mongol tribes that migrated to the Korean Peninsula from Central Asia. In the seventh century, Korea was unified for the first time under the Shilla Kingdom (now a very popular restaurant name in Korea and the Korean diaspora) and was then ruled by a royal family until Japan invaded in 1910 and instituted colonial rule. After World War II, Korea was divided into a republic in the South and a communist state in the North.

Korea abounds with fresh produce. Even though mountains cover two-thirds of the country, soils are rich and productive, and crops are grown and preserved to fit into four distinct seasons. Spring and autumn are short, summer is hot and humid, and winter is cold and dry with lots of snow.

Based on rice and vegetables, Korean cuisine was born out of hardship, but it was developed through the royal families to an art form that became part of the way of life. The five or more side dishes of fermented or fresh vegetables that accompany most meals were a way of varying a predominantly vegetarian diet. Small amounts of seafood were consumed, but meat was traditionally scarce.

Historical development

The transportation of different ingredients around the world in the days of Christopher Columbus and Marco Polo has left an indelible mark on many cuisines, and Korean dishes were no exception. Many foods that came from South America, such as tomatoes, potatoes, and chili peppers, changed the way food was prepared. Apples and watermelon also had an impact, but the introduction of chili peppers was revolutionary. Kimchi evolved from a simple vegetable fermented in salt to a more complex and delicious dish with the addition of dried red chili powder. The abundance of foods seasoned with chili peppers and the huge quantities of chili peppers and products sold in shops and markets make it difficult to believe that chili wasn't always a part of the Korean diet.

Stone kimchi storage vessels have been found from as early as the fourth century, and early written Chinese records describe Koreans as "being very good in making fermented foods such as wine, soybean paste and salted and fermented fish." During what is known as the Ancient Period (before AD 918), kimchi was made by dipping vegetables in salt, vinegar, and grain. The types of vegetables used were turnips, eggplants (aubergines), gourds, wild leeks, bamboo shoots and the roots of the Chinese bellflower.

During the Koryo Period (from 918 to 1392), Buddhists preferred vegetables over meat in their diet and many new types of vegetables came into use. Mustard greens came from India, and cucumber, garlic, lettuce, green onion, and ginger root came from China. The preparation of vegetables to last through the winter became more of a ceremony and was even celebrated in verse. There is no record of the now popular Chinese (napa) cabbage being used in this period.

The renaissance of culture and cuisine came during the Chosun Dynasty (from 1392 to 1910), when many new vegetables such as pumpkins, sweet potatoes, white gourds, apples and watermelons were cultivated. During the early part of the dynasty, the distinctive red color of kimchi, the national color of Korea, came from the cockscomb flower and safflower. That all changed around the seventeenth century when chili peppers were introduced.

Even since the end of World War II, Korea has been somewhat isolated from the rest of the world as ordinary people find it difficult to travel overseas. The result has been that the cuisine remained relatively free of outside influence until around the mid-1980s. Now big cities such as Seoul boast fast food from around the world with an emphasis on steakhouse franchises from the United States and Australia.

Food preparation

The main ingredients in Korean cuisine are salt, soybean paste, green onions, ginger, black pepper, sesame oil, sesame salt, vinegar, soy sauce, red chili paste, garlic, red chili powder, Chinese (napa) cabbage, white radish, cucumber, Indian mustard leaf, and Korean watercress stems.

Many households still make their own soy sauce, soybean paste and kimchi every year. There is an old proverb that says you can judge a person's culinary skill from the tastes of these homemade staples.

How to prepare and serve dinner

Table settings are very important in Korean meals. There are casual, everyday settings and more formal ceremonial settings. For each, all the foods are traditionally put in the center of the table at the same time so they can all be enjoyed together.

The most common daily setting is called "bansang charim," in which rice is the main dish served with numerous side dishes, or "banchan." This can be further classified as "3-cheop" up to "12-cheop," indicating the number of side dishes. During the Joseon Dynasty, social class determined how many side dishes were allowed, with nine side dishes for nobility only.

There are maps to show the traditional placement of dishes, but the everyday setting is changing as dietary habits change and women simply do not have the time to conform to the rigid settings. Serving dishes are generally low flat bowls; the chopsticks are flattened metal and take an extra bit of skill to wield successfully. Rice is served in individual bowls; never serve food over the rice before serving. One very pretty serving bowl is that for "gujeolpan," a deep, octagonal lacquered tray with eight sections around the outside and one in the middle. A variety of colored vegetables and meats is served in the eight outer sections, while the middle holds dainty, thin pancakes in which the ingredients are rolled.

The ceremonial settings are different for memorable occasions, including a baby's 100th day celebration, a first birthday, a wedding day and a sixtieth birthday.

Etiquette

Elders are served first and others wait for them to start eating. It is disrespectful to leave the table before the elders after the meal is over. The Korean meal used to be a silent affair, but now food is served communally, and conversation thrives.

Rice and soup are eaten with a spoon and side dishes with chopsticks. It is important not to use spoons and chopsticks at the same time and not to hold dishes in the hands while eating. After the meal, chopsticks and spoon are placed as they were laid out originally.

Bulgogi is a popular restaurant dish, made with marinated beef that is cooked on a griddle at the table and served wrapped in a lettuce leaf with vegetables, chili paste, green onions, and fresh slivers of garlic. The etiquette is to wrap everything in the lettuce and eat it all in one bite, but this takes some doing if the parcel is large.

There are also manners for drinking parties—for example, one pours liquor for other people only, never for oneself, and when a young person drinks with an older person, the young person will receive the liquor only when it is offered and will drink with the head turned aside, not facing the older person.

Festivals

Traditional foods are used to celebrate various festivals. The Lunar New Year is celebrated with a memorial service for the ancestors, and a rice cake soup called "tteokguk" is eaten, along with a variety of treats such as japchae noodles, mung bean pancakes and special fruit punches. It is said that eating nuts (walnuts, chestnuts or peanuts) at dawn on the day of the year's first full moon will frighten away all the bad spirits. Five-grain rice and sweet rice are also served on that day.

"Dano" is the day when the summer heat begins, and rice cakes, fish soup and punch are on the menu. "Sambok," in the searing heat of summer, is celebrated with a young chicken boiled with sticky rice, ginseng, Chinese dates and garlic. The traditional wisdom is that hot food keeps minds and bodies strong throughout the summer.

"Chuseok," the Autumnal Full Moon Harvest Festival, is celebrated by Koreans around the world. Families dressed in traditional silk "hanbok" commemorate their ancestors and prepare a rice-based banquet.

Even far from Korea, families believe that it is just as important to teach children Korean customs, as it is to teach children the Korean language. "Chuseok" is the most important family get-together of the year. In Korea, where two-thirds of the population travel to their home towns and villages, ancestors' graves are visited and tended. One of the special dishes prepared for this day is "songpyeon," a half-moon-shaped rice cake that contains sesame seeds, red beans or chestnuts.

On "Dongji," or the Winter Solstice, it is traditional to eat red bean porridge with rice balls—one rice ball for each year of your age and red beans to prevent bad luck.

Drinks

Teas have been developed to a high art in Korea. Green tea is made with leaves from tea trees that originally came from China, but other teas are made from fruits, grains and medicinal herbs. In fact, many teas are consumed for their health benefits: ginger tea is great for a cold; ginseng tea helps in recovery from fatigue and livens up the metabolism; citron tea, made from a golden marmalade substance and hot water, contains large amounts of vitamin C.

Arrowroot tea and Chinese quince tea are said to be a good treatment for bronchitis. Ginseng (insam), a long white root vegetable, is used as a restorative and tonic, and thought to strengthen vital organs, stimulate the heart, protect the stomach, enhance stamina and calm the nerves. It gives tea a slightly bitter taste and is also used whole in liquor or cooked with chicken in a stew called "Samgyetang." Barley and corn for tea-making are widely available in Korean grocery stores.

Traditional fruit drinks are served with desserts. One is a sweet fermented rice and malt drink that is served with floating pine nuts. Another is cinnamon fruit punch.

The most popular Korean liquor, "soju," is made from fermented potatoes. It is gaining a market in Japan and around the world. "Makgeolli" is unrefined rice wine, and "cheongju" is refined rice wine. An endless variety of folk liquors, some with a very high alcohol content, is made from such ingredients as azaleas, wheat, millet, sticky rice, pear, and ginger.

Equipment

Porcelain bowls

Porcelain bowls are used to serve side dishes.

Cooking and metal chopsticks

Traditional Korean chopsticks are made of stainless steel or silver. Chopsticks are normally reserved for selecting from side dishes, with spoons being used for rice and soup.

Hot pot (Ttukbaegi)

A circular clay pot with a cover, used for cooking soups and stews. It can be placed directly over a gas flame or on an electric hotplate. Its main advantage is that it can be transferred to the table, where it will keep the food hot during the meal.

Nine-section tray (Gujeolpan)

This tray contains a central section for gujeolpan pancakes (page 34) and eight surrounding sections for fillings, usually finely sliced meat and vegetables. Seven-section trays are also available.

Traditional kimchi jar (Hang-ari)

In a traditional Korean home, kimchi is stored to ferment in earthenware jars. These are located in a cool place where the temperature remains relatively even. These days, small quantities of kimchi are more likely to be stored in glass containers in the refrigerator.

Porcelain bowls

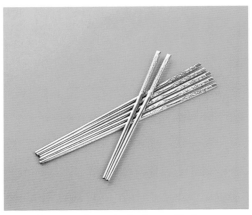

Cooking and metal chopsticks

Hot pot (Ttukbaegi)

Nine-section tray (Gujeolpan)

Traditional kimchi jar (Hang-ari)

Ingredients

Beans, mung

Beans, soy

**Chili peppers, large hot Korean
(Gochu)**

Chinese bellflower root (Doraji)

Chinese (napa) cabbage

Beans, mung
The sprouts of these small green beans are commonly used in Chinese cooking.

Beans, soy
Soybeans are valued for their high levels of protein and beneficial oils and low level of carbohydrates. Used to make tofu, soy sauce, soybean flour and soybean oil.

Chili peppers, large hot Korean
The red chili pepper, was introduced to Korea in the early seventeenth century and has been incorporated into almost every Korean dish, especially kimchi. Anaheim (long) chili peppers may be substituted.

Chinese bellflower root
Chinese bellflower root resembles ginseng and contains carbohydrates, calcium and iron as well as saponin, a major component of ginseng. The root is soaked in water before cooking to remove the bitter taste and soften the fiber.

Chinese (napa) cabbage
Chinese cabbage is a biennial indigenous to eastern Asia, and it is a basic ingredient of kimchi. It is also used for making soup and is a good source of calcium, potassium and iron.

Crown daisy leaves

A variety of chrysanthemum, these are used in Korean recipes as a kind of spinach and, with stems intact, in Asian stir-fries.

Fermented shrimp

The shrimp are mixed with salt and stored in a cool place for 2–3 months before use. Purchase ready-to-use. Keeps unrefrigerated for 1 year.

Fernbrake or fiddlehead fern

Known in Japan as "warabi." Purchase dried fernbrake and soak in warm water for 30 minutes before use. Also see Glossary, page 122.

Ginger, fresh

Fresh ginger is an important seasoning in Korean recipes and, grated, provides ginger juice. Do not substitute powdered ginger.

Ginko nuts

The ginko tree is revered in Asia for the health-giving properties of its leaves and nuts. The yellowish green kernels of the nuts taste best skewered and roasted on a grill or barbecue.

Ginseng root

Ginseng is widely cultivated in Korea, and is of the world's finest quality. Tasting similar to parsnip, it is used in soups, stews, and teas. Ginseng is believed to have properties that strengthen and rejuvenate the body.

Crown daisy leaves (Ssukgat)

Fermented shrimp (Saeujeot)

Fernbrake (Gosari)

Ginger, fresh (Saenggang)

Ginko nuts (Eunhaeng)

Ginseng root (Insam)

Green onions: Daepa (top, thick) and Jiokpa (bottom, thin)

Jellyfish strips (Haepari)

Korean watercress stems (Minari)

Kosher salt (Kulgeun sogeum)

Lentil jelly (Cheongpomuk)

Malt liquid (Mullyeot)

Green onions: Daepa and Jiokpa

Sometimes called Korean leeks, these resemble scallions (shallots/spring onions) in flavor, without the onion aroma. Substitute scallions. Also see Glossary, page 122.

Jellyfish strips

Prized for their texture rather than their taste, jellyfish strips are made from the cap of the jellyfish, which has been salted and dried. Waxy in appearance, the strips become soft and crunchy after soaking.

Korean watercress

Similar to the watercress found in most supermarkets, the Korean variety has a more pungent taste. Only the stems are used in the recipes.

Kosher salt

This coarse-grained sea salt is free of additives. Koreans believe that minerals such as iodine that are added to most table salt may alter the flavors of the foods. However, additive-free table salts are available from supermarkets.

Lentil jelly

Added to food for its chewy texture and carbohydrate content. Also see Glossary, page 122.

Malt liquid

Used to add shine to dishes. Also see Glossary, page 122.

Mushrooms

Dried Chinese mushrooms have a distinctive aroma and flavor. Although they are referred to as black, they are pale buff to brown in color. They are sold in small packs and should be stored in an airtight container after opening. Also see Glossary, page 122.

Noodles

The most common noodles used in Korean recipes are sweet potato starch or mung bean (dangmyeon), wheat (somyeon), and udon noodles. Also see Glossary, pages 122–123.

Rice cakes

These savory rice cakes are specifically used for serving with dumpling and rice cake soup (tteok manduguk), which is traditionally eaten on the first day of the new year (see recipe page 57).

Radish, Japanese daikon and Korean round

Daikon is one of the main ingredients of numerous kinds of kimchi and is believed to aid in the digestion of oily foods. Also see Glossary, page 123.

Seaweed: Nori and dried

See page 21 for information.

Mushrooms (left to right): Dried Chinese, Enoki, Shiitake (Pyogo)

Noodles (left to right): Dangmyeon, Udon (Udong), Somyeon, Soba

Rice cakes (Huin tteok)

Radish (left to right): Japanese daikon and Korean round (Mu)

Seaweed: Nori (Gim)

Seaweed: Dried

Seaweed: Kelp (Miyeok)

Shiso/perilla leaves (Kkaennip)

Soy sauce, Korean (Ganjang)

Sticky (glutinous) rice

Tofu (Dubu)

Seaweed: Nori, Dried and Kelp

Korean recipes call for nori, dried and kelp seaweed. Nori is sold as paper-thin, dried, flat square sheets and is shredded and added to soups. Dried seaweed is available crumbled in plastic bags, ready for use in soups and vegetable dishes. Kelp, also known as "kombu" or "konbu," is dark-brown seaweed that is sold in folded sheets. Lightly wipe salty mold from surface before using; do not wash.

Shiso/perilla leaves

These green, jagged-edged leaves are part of the mint and basil family. Also see Glossary, page 123.

Soy sauce

There are two kinds of soy sauces in Korean cooking: the light Japanese variety and Korean soy sauce (chosun soy sauce), which is brownish black, not sweet and used for soups.

Sticky (glutinous) rice

This oval-grained white rice is used almost exclusively for sweets in Korean cooking. It is also available as a powder.

Tofu

Korean tofu is made by boiling ground mung beans with water. It is used in soups, stir-fries, stews, sauces, and dips.

Ingredients

16 oz (500 g) Korean round radish, cut into bite-sized pieces

2 lb (1 kg) Chinese (napa) cabbage, cut into bite-sized pieces

$\frac{1}{2}$ cup (4 oz/125 g) kosher or sea salt

1 oz (30 g) jjokpa or scallion (shallot/spring onion), white portion only

1 clove garlic

1 small knob fresh ginger, about $\frac{1}{3}$ oz (10 g)

2 hot red chili peppers

1 oz (30 g) Korean watercress stems (minari)

4 oz (125 g) nashi or other firm pear

4 oz (125 g) medium yellow (brown) onion

20 cups (16 fl oz/5 L) water

5 tablespoons hot red chili powder

KIMCHI

Watery radish kimchi

Nabak kimchi

Place radish and Chinese cabbage in a large glass or ceramic bowl. Sprinkle with $\frac{1}{4}$ cup (2 oz/60 g) of the salt and let stand for 15–20 minutes, tossing occasionally so salt penetrates vegetables.

Roughly chop jjokpa, garlic, ginger, and chili peppers. Remove and discard leaves from watercress stems and cut stems into $1\frac{1}{2}$-inch (3-cm) lengths.

Rinse radish and cabbage in cold water to remove salt. Drain, then place in a large bowl. Add pear, onion, jjokpa, garlic, ginger, chili peppers and watercress stems. Mix thoroughly, then transfer to a 20-cup (160-fl oz/5-L) kimchi container (clay or glass, with a lid).

Pour water into large bowl and stir in remaining salt. Wrap chili powder in a clean cloth, tie to make a bundle and immerse in salted water. Stir cloth in the water until chili powder turns water red. Remove and discard bundle. Pour chili water into kimchi container. Cover and leave in a cool place for 3–4 days before using. The unused portion can be stored in the refrigerator for about 5 days.

Makes about 30 cups (240 fl oz/7.5 L)

Hint
If you do not wish to prepare your own, watery radish kimchi is readily available from Korean markets.

Note
Due to recent changes in the romanization of Korean words, kimchi is also written as "gimchi."

Chinese cabbage kimchi

Baechu kimchi

1. Remove outer leaves from cabbage. Reserve a few leaves, then cut cabbages in half lengthwise. Combine kosher salt and water in a large container. Add cabbage halves and allow to soak until tender, 6–8 hours. Remove cabbage from the salted water, rinse, then squeeze out excess water.

2. Slice daikon into matchstick-sized pieces. Cut ijokpa, mustard leaves (if using) and watercress stems into 1¹/₂-inch (4-cm) lengths and combine with daikon in a large bowl. Peel garlic, ginger and onion. Cut chili peppers lengthwise and remove cores and seeds. Combine garlic, ginger, onion and peppers with ¹/₂ cup (4 oz/ 125 ml) water in a food processor. Blend to a paste, then combine with daikon mixture.

3. Mix shrimp and anchovies with chili powder. Add sticky rice liquid, table salt and sugar, and mix well. Add to daikon mixture and toss to combine.

4. Using your fingers, separate leaves of the cabbage halves and spoon some of chili pepper mixture between each. Place filled leaves in a kimchi container (clay or glass, with a lid), cover with one reserved large cabbage leaf or plastic wrap, then lid, and store in a cool place for 2–3 days to mature before using. Store any unused kimchi in the refrigerator for up to 1 week.

Ingredients

- 2 large Chinese (napa) cabbages
- 4 cups (1 lb/1 kg) kosher (sea) salt
- 20 cups (160 fl oz/5 L) water
- 20 oz (625 g) daikon
- 2 oz (60 g) ijokpa or scallions (shallots/spring onions)
- 3 oz (90 g) mustard leaves (optional)
- 4 oz (125 g) Korean watercress stems (minari)
- 2 whole bulbs garlic
- 2 small knobs (about the size of a garlic bulb) fresh ginger
- 1 small yellow (brown) onion
- 10 fresh red chili peppers
- ¹/₂ cup (4 oz/125 g) fermented shrimp
- ¹/₂ cup (4 oz/125 g) fermented anchovies
- 2 cups (10 oz/300 g) red chili powder
- 1 oz (30 g) sticky rice powder dissolved in 1¹/₂ cups (12 fl oz/375 ml) water
- 1 cup (8 oz/250 g) table salt
- ¹/₄ cup (2 oz/60 g) sugar

1

2

3

4

Ingredients

10 gherkin cucumbers (joseon oi)

½ cup (4 oz/ 125 g) kosher or sea salt

1 cup (8 oz/250 g) table salt

3 oz (90 g) chives

2 oz (60 g) jjokpa or scallions (shallots/spring onions)

1 medium nashi (bae) or other firm pear

1 clove garlic

1 small knob fresh ginger, about ⅓ oz (10 g)

¼ cup (2 fl oz/60 ml) fermented shrimp (optional)

4 tablespoons hot red chili powder

1 tablespoon sugar

½ teaspoon salt

Stuffed cucumber
Oi sobaegi

Smooth cucumber skins by rubbing with kosher salt. Cut off and discard the top and bottom ½ inch (1 cm) and cut cucumbers into sections measuring 2 inches (5 cm) long. Make a slit down one side of each section, cutting to within ½ inch (12 mm) of the ends of each section. Turn cucumber 90 degrees and make a second slit. Add salt to a medium bowl of water, and place cucumber sections in bowl. Leave until soft, 1–2 hours.

Roughly chop chives, jjokpa and pear. Finely chop garlic, ginger and shrimp. Combine chives, jjokpa, pear, garlic, ginger, shrimp, chili powder and sugar in a large bowl. Mix well. Gently squeeze excess water from cucumber sections. Dry with paper towels, then fill with shrimp mixture. Reserve bowl.

Place stuffed cucumbers in a 6-cup (48 fl oz/1.5-L) kimchi container (clay or glass, with a lid). Pour ½ cup (4 fl oz/125 ml) water into reserved bowl, add ½ teaspoon of salt and pour over cucumbers. Let cucumbers stand overnight, then store until ready to use. The cucumber will keep in the refrigerator for about 5 days.

Makes 10 cucumbers

White **Chinese cabbage** kimchi

Baek kimchi

Cut cabbage in half lengthwise. Combine salt and stock in a large bowl, then add cabbage. Soak for 6–8 hours in warm weather or 8–12 hours in cold weather. Remove cabbage from water and rinse several times in cold water. Shake off excess water.

Slice daikon into thin strips. Cut jiokpa, watercress stems, and mustard leaves into 1–1½-inch (2.5–4-cm) lengths. Peel and core pear. Remove skins from chestnuts and pit dates. Finely slice pear, chestnuts and dates.

If using dried Chinese mushrooms, drain off water then remove and discard stems. Thinly slice shiitake mushrooms or Chinese mushroom caps. Crush garlic and ginger. Mix all ingredients, including fermented shrimp, except the cabbage leaves and stock, in a large bowl.

Using your fingers, separate cabbage leaves and spoon some of chili pepper mixture between each. Place filled leaves in a kimchi container (clay or glass, with a lid), cover with one large cabbage leaf or a piece of plastic wrap and then the lid, and store in a cool place for 3–4 days to mature before use. Then store in the refrigerator.

Ingredients

- 1 Chinese (napa) cabbage
- 2 cups (1 lb/500 g) kosher or sea salt
- 2 cups (16 fl oz/500 ml) beef stock or water
- 3 oz (90 g) daikon
- 3 oz (90 g) jiokpa or scallions (shallots/spring onions)
- 4 oz (125 g) Korean watercress stems (minari)
- 2 oz (60 g) mustard leaves
- 4 oz (125 g) pear (preferably nashi)
- 5 chestnuts
- 5 dried dates
- 5 shiitake or dried Chinese mushrooms soaked for 30 minutes in several changes of water
- 1 whole bulb garlic
- 1 small knob fresh ginger, about ⅓ oz (10 g)
- ½ cup (4 oz/125 g) fermented shrimp
- pinch shredded hot red chili pepper
- 2 tablespoons sugar
- 2 cups (16 fl oz/500 ml) water

APPETIZERS

Korean mung bean pancakes

Nokdu bindaetteok

1. Soak mung beans in water overnight to soften.

2. Using your hands, rub soaked beans together to remove skins. Remove skins when they float to the surface of water.

3. Transfer beans to a food processor and blend to a paste with extra water. Add sticky rice powder and mix with a spoon.

4. Finely slice yellow onion and cabbage. Sprinkle with salt and leave for about 15 minutes to sweat (do not rinse off salt).

5. Cut white parts of daepa into fine strips.

6. Mix pork with onion, cabbage, scallion and garlic.

7. Add mung bean paste and mix to combine. Add salt to taste.

8. Heat 1 tablespoon oil in a frying pan. Ladle enough bean mixture into pan to make an 8-inch (20-cm) pancake. Cook until golden brown, about 3 minutes on each side.

To make dipping sauce: Combine soy sauce and white vinegar in a bowl.

Transfer pancakes to a plate and serve whole or sliced, accompanied by dipping sauce. Serve immediately. If pancake cools, reheat in heated frying pan for about 1 minute on each side.

Makes 15 pancakes

Ingredients

2 cups (14 oz/440 g) mung beans

water for soaking

3 cups (24 fl oz/750 ml) extra water

⅓ cup (1½ oz/45 g) sticky rice powder

1½ oz (45 g) yellow (brown) onion

1 oz (30 g) Chinese (napa) cabbage kimchi

1 teaspoon table salt

5 daepa or scallions (shallots/spring onions), white parts only

2 oz (60 g) ground (minced) pork fillet

1 tablespoon crushed garlic

1 tablespoon finely chopped scallions (shallots/spring onions)

vegetable or sunflower oil for frying

FOR DIPPING SAUCE

2 teaspoons light soy sauce

1 teaspoon white vinegar

Ingredients

1 block green lentil jelly, about 24 oz (750 g)

4 oz (125 g) beef tenderloin or scotch fillet, sliced into 1½-inch (4-cm) strips

vegetable or sunflower oil for frying

1 egg, separated

4 oz (125 g) bean sprouts, washed and trimmed

1 sheet nori (gim), 7½ x 8 inches (19 x 20½ cm), cut into thin strips

4 oz (125 g) Korean watercress (minari), stems only, cut into 1½-inch (4-cm) lengths

pinch dried hot red chili pepper, julienned, for garnish (optional)

FOR BEEF MARINADE

1 tablespoon light soy sauce

2 teaspoons sugar

1 teaspoon minced garlic

1 teaspoon sesame oil

1 teaspoon pan-toasted, ground sesame seeds

freshly ground black pepper, to taste

FOR SEASONING

4½ teaspoons Korean soy sauce

4½ teaspoons white vinegar

1 teaspoon sugar

Green lentil jelly
Tangpyeongchae

Slice jelly into pieces about 1½ inches (4 cm) long and ½ inch (12 mm) wide. Set aside.

To make beef marinade: Combine marinade ingredients in a medium glass or ceramic bowl.

Place beef strips in marinade and leave to marinate for 10–15 minutes. Heat 2–3 drops of oil in a nonstick frying pan. Add marinated beef strips (no need to drain) and stir-fry over medium heat until cooked through, 3–4 minutes. Turn off heat, leaving meat in the pan to keep warm. Discard marinade.

Fry egg white and yolk to make egg gidan (see step 9, page 42). Remove from pan and cut into thin strips. Set aside a small amount for garnish.

Plunge bean sprouts into a small saucepan of boiling salted water for about 1 minute. Remove and drain.

To make seasoning: In a bowl combine seasoning ingredients and mix well.

Carefully combine jelly, beef and bean sprouts in a large bowl. Sprinkle with seasoning mixture, garnish with reserved egg gidan and chili pepper strips and serve.

Alternatively, place jelly pieces in center of a serving platter and arrange other ingredients individually around them for diners to help themselves. Accompany with seasoning mixture, served in a separate bowl.

Serves 4

Jellyfish with vegetables

Haepari naengchae

Rinse jellyfish several times in cold water to remove the salt. Heat water to boiling in a small saucepan. Using a metal strainer, plunge jellyfish into boiling water for a few seconds, then transfer to a bowl of cold water and leave for about 10 minutes. This process softens jellyfish and gives it a milder taste.

Cut cucumber into 2-inch (5-cm) lengths. Using a peeler, peel off the skin in lengthwise strips. Discard whitish flesh and cut strips into matchstick-sized slices.

Refresh lettuce leaves in cold water, then drain.

To make mustard and garlic sauce: Warm beef stock in a small saucepan. Add mustard powder and stir to dissolve. Add sugar, vinegar, salt, and garlic and stir until sugar and salt dissolve.

Arrange lettuce leaves, lemon and parsley stems on a serving plate. Place cucumber slices, shrimp and jellyfish in center of lettuce leaves. Pour sauce over all ingredients. Add lemon juice to shrimp and jellyfish and mix to coat immediately before serving.

Serves 4 or 5

Ingredients

- 10 oz (300 g) jellyfish strips preserved in salt (haepari)
- 2 cups (16 fl oz/500 ml) water
- 1 medium cucumber
- 4 lettuce leaves
- ½ lemon
- 4 parsley stems cut into 1½-inch (4-cm) lengths
- 4 medium-sized cooked shrimp (prawns)
- 2 tablespoons fresh lemon juice

FOR MUSTARD AND GARLIC SAUCE
- 3 tablespoons beef stock or water
- 1 tablespoon mild or hot dry mustard
- 3 tablespoons sugar
- 3 tablespoons white vinegar
- 2 teaspoons kosher or sea salt
- 1 teaspoon ground (minced) garlic

Ingredients

4 oz (125 g) beef tenderloin or scotch fillet, sliced into thin 1½-inch (4-cm) strips

5 dried Chinese mushrooms, soaked for about 30 minutes in several changes of water

vegetable or sunflower oil for frying

5 oz (150 g) button mushrooms, stems removed, caps thinly sliced

1 medium cucumber

4 oz (125 g) julienned carrot strips, about 1½ inches (4 cm) long

5 oz (150 g) bean sprouts

salt and freshly ground black pepper

sesame oil

3 eggs, separated

1 teaspoon pan-toasted pine nuts, cut in half

FOR CREPES
1 cup (4 oz/125 g) all-purpose (plain) flour

½ teaspoon table salt

1¼ cups (10 fl oz/300 ml) water

FOR BEEF MARINADE
2 tablespoons light soy sauce

1 tablespoon sugar

2 tablespoons finely chopped scallions (shallots/spring onions)

1 tablespoon minced garlic

2 teaspoons sesame oil

2 teaspoons pan-toasted, ground sesame seeds

freshly ground black pepper to taste

FOR SOUR SOY SAUCE
3 tablespoons light soy sauce

4½ teaspoons white vinegar

1 tablespoon water

Gujeolpan

To make crepes: Sift flour and salt together into a bowl. Add water gradually to form a batter, and let stand while preparing the fillings.

To make marinade: In a glass bowl, combine marinade ingredients.

Squeeze excess water from Chinese mushrooms. Remove stems and slice caps thinly. Marinate beef and mushrooms separately for 20 minutes.

Heat 1 tablespoon oil in a frying pan. Stir-fry beef over high heat for 2–3 minutes. Remove from pan and set aside on paper towels. Clean pan, add ½ tablespoon oil and stir-fry dried mushrooms over high heat for 1 minute. Remove and drain on paper towels. Add 1 tablespoon oil and fry button mushrooms for 1 minute; remove and drain on paper towels.

Cut cucumber into 1½-inch (4-cm) lengths. Peel off thick strips of skin (include some white flesh), then cut into thin strips (discard cucumber flesh). Transfer cucumber strips to a bowl of salted water and leave for 4 minutes. Remove from bowl and squeeze out excess water.

In a lightly oiled frying pan, fry carrot strips for 1 minute. Drain on paper towels and let cool. Fry cucumber for about 30 seconds. Plunge bean sprouts in boiling salted water for about 30 seconds. Remove from water, let cool then gently squeeze out excess water. Season with a pinch of salt and pepper and sesame oil to taste. Set aside.

Fry egg white and yolk to make egg gidan (see step 9, page 42). Remove from pan and cut into thin strips.

Heat a little oil in a frying pan, then spoon in about 1 tablespoon of the crepe batter. Cook until off-white, about 1 minute on each side; do not allow to brown. Remove from pan and repeat with remaining batter. Stack crepes in the center of a gujeolpan dish, sprinkling halved pine nuts between each crepe.

To make sour soy sauce: In a small bowl, mix sour soy sauce ingredients.

Arrange filling ingredients in containers or individually around the crepes. Provide guests with small plates and teaspoons for the sauce. Diners place a crepe on their plate, spoon on a little sauce, then top with their choice of fillings. Crepes are rolled up and eaten with the fingers.

Serves 4

Pine nut **porridge**
Jatjuk

Ingredients

½ cup (4 oz/125 g) pine nuts

5 cups (40 fl oz/1.25 L) water

1 cup (8 oz/250 g) medium-grain rice, soaked for about 30 minutes, drained

table salt to taste (optional)

Place pine nuts in blender with 1 cup (8 fl oz/250 ml) water and blend to combine. Remove and set aside. Wash out blender container.

Place rice in blender with 1 cup (8 fl oz/250 ml) water and blend to a coarse paste. Transfer to a nonstick saucepan, add remaining water and cook, stirring occasionally, over medium heat for 15 minutes. Reduce heat to low, add pine nut liquid and simmer, uncovered, for a further 15 minutes. Ladle into serving bowls and allow diners to add salt to taste.

Serves 4 or 5

Mung bean **porridge**
Nokdujuk

Ingredients

1 cup (8 oz/250 g) mung beans, soaked in water for 2 hours, drained

12 cups (96 fl oz/3 L) water

1 cup (8 oz/250 g) medium-grain rice, soaked in water for 30 minutes, drained

table salt to taste (optional)

Place mung beans and 8 cups (64 fl oz/2 L) of water in a large saucepan and bring a boil. Boil until beans are soft, 20–30 minutes. Drain, reserving cooking water. Transfer beans to a blender. Blend beans to a paste, gradually adding cooking water.

Bring soaked rice and remaining water to a boil in a large nonstick saucepan, stirring occasionally. Lower heat to medium and add mung bean paste. Reduce heat to simmer and cook, uncovered, until rice becomes soggy, about 20 minutes. Ladle porridge into bowls and allow diners to add salt to taste.

Serves 4 or 5

Soybean **porridge**

Kongjuk

Ingredients

½ cup (4 oz/125 g) soybeans, soaked in water for 5–6 hours, drained

1 cup (8 oz/250 g) medium-grain rice, soaked in water for about 30 minutes, drained

table salt to taste (optional)

Place soybeans in a medium-sized saucepan, cover with water and bring to a boil. Remove from heat and rinse in bowl of cold water. When soybeans have cooled sufficiently, rub them together with your hands to remove transparent husks (they will float to the surface). Pour out water and repeat process until all husks are removed. Transfer soybeans to a blender, add 1 cup (8 fl oz/250 ml) water and blend to combine to a paste. Remove mixture from blender and set aside.

Place rice in a medium-sized saucepan, cover with water and bring to a boil. Remove from heat and rinse in cold water. Drain and transfer to a blender. Add 1 cup (8 fl oz/250 ml) water and blend to a smooth paste.

Pour soybean mixture into a medium-sized saucepan and bring to a boil. Cook for about 5 minutes, then add rice mixture and 4 cups (32 fl oz/1 L) water. Reduce to a simmer and cook uncovered for a further 20 minutes. Ladle into bowls and serve sprinkled with salt.

Serves 4 or 5

Abalone porridge

Jeonbokjuk

Ingredients

4 oz (125 g) fresh abalone, washed and cleaned with a brush

1 cup (8 oz/250 g) medium-grain rice, soaked in water for about 30 minutes, drained

6 cups (48 fl oz/1.5 L) water

2 tablespoons sesame oil

table salt to taste (optional)

Slice abalone into thin strips 1 inch (2 cm) long. Set aside. Place rice in a blender with 1 cup (8 fl oz/250 ml) water and blend to a coarse paste. Heat sesame oil in a nonstick frying pan. Add abalone strips and rice paste, and cook, stirring, for 15 minutes. Add remaining water and bring to a boil. Reduce heat to low and simmer until most of the liquid is absorbed, 20–30 minutes. Add salt to taste just before serving.

Serves 4 or 5

Red bean porridge
Patjuk

Wash red beans, then drain. Bring a medium-size saucepan of water to a boil, add red beans and cook until soft, about 30 minutes. Drain beans, reserving water, and mash with a fork or potato masher. Press through a fine sieve into a medium-sized bowl, diluting mashed bean mixture from time to time with 5 cups (40 fl oz/1.25 L) water to help it through the sieve and separate bean skin from flesh. Discard bean skins from sieve.

Add reserved bean water to bean puree. This creates a two-layered effect, with heavy bean mixture on the bottom and water on top.

Carefully pour bean water into a medium-sized saucepan, add soaked rice and bring to a boil. Reduce to simmer and cook, covered, until soft, about 20 minutes. Add bean paste and cook uncovered, for 10–15 minutes longer, stirring occasionally with a wooden spoon.

To make rice balls: Combine sticky rice powder, hot water and pinch of salt in a small bowl. Using your hands, form mixture into marble-sized balls. Bring a medium-sized saucepan of water to a boil. Add rice balls and cook until they rise to the surface, 1–2 minutes. Remove from saucepan and wash in cold water.

Add rice balls to the bean and rice mixture and bring to a boil to heat through.

Serve porridge hot in bowls, sprinkled with salt and sugar to taste.

Serves 4 or 5

Ingredients

1 cup (7 oz/220 g) dried red beans

1 cup (8 oz/250 g) medium-grain rice, soaked for about 30 minutes, drained

table salt to taste (optional)

sugar to taste (optional)

FOR RICE BALLS

1 cup (7 oz/220 g) sticky rice powder

2 tablespoons hot water

pinch table salt

Ingredients

2 oz (60 g) red radish, cut into thin strips about 1½ inches (4 cm) long

2 oz (60 g) radish (mu), cut into thin strips about 1½ inches (4 cm) long

2 oz (60 g) carrots, cut into thin strips about 1½ inches (4 cm) long

2 oz (60 g) cucumber, cut into thin strips about 1½ inches (4 cm) long

4 shiso (kkaennip) leaves, cut into thin strips about 1½ inches (4 cm) long

2 oz (60 g) lettuce leaves, cut into thin strips about 1½ inches (4 cm) long

4 oz (125 g) beef tenderloin or scotch fillet, cut into thin strips about 1½ inches (4 cm) long

4 servings hot steamed (medium-grain) rice

4 fried eggs

FOR BEEF MARINADE

1 tablespoon light soy sauce

1½ teaspoons sugar

2 teaspoons finely chopped scallions (shallots/spring onions)

1 teaspoon crushed garlic

1 teaspoon pan-toasted, ground sesame seeds

1 teaspoon sesame oil

pinch black pepper

FOR HOT RED CHILI PASTE SAUCE

2 tablespoons hot red chili paste

3 tablespoons beef stock

2 tablespoons sugar

1 tablespoon sesame oil

1 tablespoon pan-toasted, ground sesame seeds

Fresh vegetable bibimbap

Sanchae bibimbap

Freshen red radish, radish, carrots, cucumber, shiso leaves and lettuce by dipping them separately in cold water, then draining.

To make beef marinade: Combine marinade ingredients in a glass or ceramic bowl.

Add beef to marinade and marinate for 10 minutes. Heat 1 teaspoon vegetable oil in a frying pan and stir-fry beef over medium heat until well done, 3–5 minutes.

To make chili paste sauce: Mix chili paste sauce ingredients together and spoon into a serving bowl.

To serve, divide rice among 4 bowls, arrange beef and vegetables over rice, and top with a fried egg. Serve chili paste sauce in separate bowls and allow each diner to mix sauce into their own bowls of bibimbap.

Serves 4

Tip
You can use any vegetables you like. Seasonal vegetables are best.

Note: Traditionally, the ingredients are arranged over the rice in grouped vertical segments, and then topped with an egg.

Ingredients

2 oz (60 g) red radish, cut into thin strips about 1½ inches (4 cm) long

2 oz (60 g) radish (mu), cut into thin strips about 1½ inches (4 cm) long

2 oz (60 g) carrots, cut into thin strips about 1½ inches (4 cm) long

2 oz (60 g) cucumber, cut into thin strips about 1½ inches (4 cm) long

4 shiso (kkaennip) leaves, cut into thin strips about 1½ inches (4 cm) long

2 oz (60 g) lettuce leaves, cut into thin strips about 1½ inches (4 cm) long

4 oz (125 g) beef tenderloin or scotch fillet, cut into thin strips about 1½ inches (4 cm) long

4 servings hot steamed (medium-grain) rice

4 fried eggs

FOR BEEF MARINADE

1 tablespoon light soy sauce

1½ teaspoons sugar

2 teaspoons finely chopped scallions (shallots/spring onions)

1 teaspoon crushed garlic

1 teaspoon pan-toasted, ground sesame seeds

1 teaspoon sesame oil

pinch black pepper

FOR HOT RED CHILI PASTE SAUCE

2 tablespoons hot red chili paste

3 tablespoons beef stock

2 tablespoons sugar

1 tablespoon sesame oil

1 tablespoon pan-toasted, ground sesame seeds

Bibimbap

1. One day in advance, rub bellflower root with salt and leave overnight. Slice beef into thin strips 1½ inches (4 cm) long. Squeeze excess water from mushrooms, remove and discard stems and cut caps into thin slices.

To make marinade: Combine marinade ingredients in a bowl.

Marinate mushrooms and beef slices separately in glass or ceramic bowls for 20 minutes.

2. Heat 1 tablespoon oil in a frying pan and fry mushrooms over high heat for 2–3 minutes. Remove from pan, heat 1½ teaspoons oil and stir-fry beef over high heat until evenly browned, about 3 minutes.

3. Cut cucumber in half lengthwise, then cut into diagonal slices about 1½ inches (4 cm) long. Sprinkle with salt and leave for 10 minutes to sweat. Squeeze out water. Heat ½ teaspoon oil in a frying pan and fry cucumber pieces over high heat for 1–2 minutes. Remove from pan and drain on paper towels.

4. Rinse salted bellflower root, then drain well and cut into thin strips.

5. Remove thick stem of fernbrake and cut remaining section into 1½-inch (4-cm) lengths.

6. Place bean sprouts in a medium-sized saucepan of boiling water and cover with a lid. Return water to a boil and cook until bean sprouts are wilted, 1–2 minutes. Remove from pan and drain.

To make vegetable seasoning: Combine seasoning ingredients, then divide among 3 small bowls.

7. Heat 2 teaspoons oil in a frying pan. Dip Chinese bellflower root and fernbrake separately into the vegetable seasoning. Fry separately over high heat until cooked, about 3 minutes. Fry bellflower root first.

8. Mix bean sprouts with any leftover vegetable seasoning.

9. Soak 2 paper towels in a small amount of oil and wipe frying pan. Fry egg white and yolk separately, tilting pan to create a pancake. Remove from pan and slice thinly to make egg gee-dan (thinly fried egg used for garnish).

10. Heat 1 cup (8 fl oz/250 g) oil in a large frying pan until very hot. Using chopsticks or tongs, dip sheet of dried kelp in oil and fry for 1 second. Remove and drain on paper towels until cool. Using your hands, crush the sheet into small pieces.

11. Place a serving of hot steamed rice in each bowl. Top with some beef, mushrooms, cucumber, fernbrake, bellflower, bean sprouts and egg gidan. Sprinkle with crushed kelp and serve. Accompany with separate bowls of chili paste and sesame oil for diners to help themselves.

Serves 4

1

2

3

4

5

6

7

8

9

10

11

Hot noodles
Onmyeon

Place beef in a large saucepan with water, scallion and garlic. Bring to a boil, lower to simmer and cook until beef is tender, about 30 minutes. Remove beef from liquid, reserving liquid, and cut into ½-inch (12-mm) thick slices. Add salt and soy sauce to broth to taste.

Fry egg whites and yolks to make egg gee-dan (see step 9, page 42). Remove from pan and cut into thin strips. Set aside to use as garnish.

Cut zucchini or cucumber in half lengthwise, remove the seeds, then slice into thin strips. Sprinkle strips with salt and leave for 10 minutes to sweat. Squeeze out excess water, then fry for about 1 minute in 1 tablespoon oil.

Squeeze excess water from Chinese mushrooms. Remove and discard stems. Slice caps thinly, then fry in 1 teaspoon oil over high heat for 1 minute.

Bring a medium saucepan of water to a boil and add noodles, stirring to prevent the noodles from sticking together. Cook until soft, about 3 minutes. Remove noodles from water and rinse several times in cold water until water is clear. Drain and divide into 4 bowls.

Top noodles with beef slices and garnish with egg gee-dan, zucchini or cucumber, mushrooms and chili pepper (if desired). Gently pour some broth into each bowl and serve.

Serves 4

Ingredients

10 oz (300 g) piece stewing (gravy) beef

15 cups (120 fl oz/3.75 L) water

1 scallion (shallot/spring onion)

3 cloves garlic

table salt to taste

light soy sauce to taste

vegetable or sunflower oil for frying

2 eggs, separated

1 medium zucchini (courgette) or cucumber

4 dried Chinese mushrooms, soaked for 30 minutes in several changes of water

10 oz (300 g) somyeon (thin, dried, wheat) noodles

dried hot red chili pepper, chopped, for garnish (optional)

Ingredients

3 dried Chinese mushrooms, soaked for 30 minutes in several changes of water

4 oz (125 g) beef tenderloin or scotch fillet, cut into thin strips, about 1½ inches (4 cm) long

vegetable or sunflower oil for frying

1 small cucumber (preferably Joseon)

table salt

2 eggs, separated

10 oz (300 g) somyeon (thin, dried wheat noodles)

1 hot red chili pepper, cut into thin strips (optional)

FOR CHILI PEPPER SAUCE
2 tablespoons chili paste

3 tablespoons Korean soy sauce

2 tablespoons sugar

1 tablespoon sesame oil

1 tablespoon pan-toasted, ground sesame seeds

FOR BEEF MARINADE
1 tablespoon light soy sauce

1½ teaspoons sugar

2 teaspoons finely chopped scallions (shallots/spring onions)

1 teaspoon crushed garlic

1 teaspoon pan-toasted, ground sesame seeds

1 teaspoon sesame oil

freshly ground black pepper to taste

Bibimmyeon

To make chili pepper sauce: In a bowl, combine chili pepper sauce ingredients and mix well, then spoon into a serving bowl.

Squeeze water from soaked mushrooms. Remove and discard stems, and cut caps into thin slices.

To make beef marinade: In a glass or ceramic bowl, combine marinade ingredients.

Add beef and mushrooms and marinate for 20–30 minutes.

Heat 1 tablespoon oil to very hot in a frying pan. Stir-fry beef and mushrooms together until browned on all sides, about 3 minutes. Remove from pan and set aside.

Cut cucumber in half lengthwise, then cut diagonally into thin slices. Sprinkle with salt and set aside for 10 minutes to sweat. Squeeze out excess water, then fry in 1 teaspoon oil over high heat for 2–3 minutes. Remove from pan and set aside.

Fry egg whites and yolks separately to make egg gidan (see step 9, page 42). Set aside.

Bring pan of water to a boil, then add noodles, stirring to prevent them from sticking together. Cook until soft, about 3 minutes. Remove noodles from water and rinse several times in cold water until water is clear. Drain.

Place noodles and chili pepper sauce in a large bowl and mix well to coat. Add beef, mushrooms and most of the cucumber (reserving a small amount as garnish) and mix well.

Serve noodles in individual bowls, topped with egg gidan, remaining cucumber and strips of hot red chili pepper.

Serves 4

Note: "Bibim" means mixed and "myeon" means noodles.

Cold noodles

Naengmyeon

Place beef in a large saucepan with water, daepa, and garlic. Bring to a boil, reduce heat to simmer and cook until liquid has reduced by two-thirds, 30–40 minutes.

Remove beef from pan, and wrap in a clean cotton or linen towel. Place a heavy weight, such as a large can on a cutting board, on top of beef and set aside. Allow stock to cool, then skim fat from surface.

Cut radish in half lengthwise, then cut into half-moon slices. Cut cucumber in half lengthwise, then cut into half-moon slices and sprinkle with salt. Leave for 5 minutes to sweat. Squeeze out water, then fry cucumber in 1 teaspoon oil until soft, about 30 seconds. Remove from pan and set aside

Peel and core pear, then cut into thick slices. Boil eggs for about 5 minutes, rolling them from time to time so yolk stays in center. Cool under cold water, peel and slice in half. Remove weight from beef, unwrap and cut into slices ½-inch (1-cm) thick slices.

Combine liquid from dongchimi kimchi with beef stock. Add salt, sugar and vinegar, adjusting quantities to taste. Set aside to continue cooling then refrigerate for about 30 minutes.

Bring a medium saucepan of water to a vigorous boil, add noodles and cook for about 2 minutes, stirring to separate. Remove from pan and rinse several times in cold water until water is clear. Drain, then divide among 4 servings bowls.

Garnish each serving with radish, cucumber, pear, beef slices and half an egg. Carefully pour the cold stock over noodles. Serve accompanied by small bowls of mustard, sugar and vinegar for diners to help themselves.

Serves 4

Ingredients

10 oz (300 g) piece stewing (gravy) beef

15 cups (120 fl oz/3.75 L) water

1 daepa or scallion (shallot/ spring onion)

3 cloves garlic

1 fermented radish from dongchimi kimchi (see Glossary, page 122)

1 small cucumber (preferably chosun or gherkin cucumber)

vegetable or sunflower oil for frying

1 pear (preferably nashi)

2 eggs

5 cups (40 fl oz/1.25 L) liquid from dongchimi kimchi or 2 packets instant soup from the buckwheat noodle pack dissolved in 5 cups (40 fl oz/1.25 L) water

1 tablespoon table salt

2 tablespoons sugar

2 tablespoons white vinegar

17 oz (520 g) naengmyeon (buckwheat) noodles

hot mustard

sugar

white vinegar for serving

Ingredients

4 dried Chinese mushrooms, soaked for about 30 minutes in several changes of water

4 oz (125 g) beef tenderloin or scotch fillet, cut into thin strips about 1½ inches (4 cm) long

vegetable or sunflower oil for frying

4 oz (125 g) spinach

4 oz (125 g) carrot, peeled, cut into thin 1½-inch (4-cm) long strips

1 egg, separated

salt and freshly ground black pepper

1 small yellow (brown) onion

2 oz (60 g) dangmyeon (sweet-potato starched noodles)

1 teaspoon pine nuts, for garnish

pan-toasted, ground sesame seeds

BEEF & MUSHROOM MARINADE
2 tablespoons light soy sauce

1 tablespoon sugar

4 teaspoons finely chopped scallions (shallots/spring onions)

2 teaspoons crushed garlic

2 teaspoons sesame oil

FOR SPINACH MARINADE
2 teaspoons finely chopped scallions (shallots/spring onions)

1 teaspoon crushed garlic

2 teaspoons sesame oil

2 teaspoons pan-toasted, ground sesame seeds

freshly ground black pepper to taste

FOR NOODLE SEASONING
1 tablespoon Korean soy sauce

1 tablespoon sugar

1 tablespoon sesame oil

Japchae

Squeeze excess water from mushrooms, then remove and discard stems. Cut caps into thin slices.

To make beef and mushroom marinade: Combine beef and mushroom marinade ingredients in a glass or ceramic bowl.

Add beef and mushroom slices and marinate for about 20 minutes.

Heat 1 tablespoon oil in a frying pan. Add beef and mushroom slices and stir-fry until well cooked, 3–4 minutes. Remove from pan and set aside on paper towels.

Wash spinach, then remove and discard roots, reserving leaves and stems. (If spinach stems are too long, cut them into 2 sections.) Immerse reserved spinach briefly in rapidly boiling salted water. Quickly remove from water and drain. Squeeze out excess water.

To prepare and use spinach marinade: In a bowl, combine spinach marinade ingredients, add spinach and set aside.

Clean frying pan. Soak 2 paper towels in a small amount of oil and use them to wipe frying pan. Heat frying pan and stir-fry carrot. In another frying pan, fry egg white and yolk to make egg gidan (see step 9, page 42). Remove from pan and cut into thin slices. Add salt and pepper to taste.

Peel onion, cut in half vertically, then thinly slice. Heat 1 teaspoon oil in a frying pan and fry onion slices, adding salt and pepper to taste.

Bring a medium saucepan of water to a boil, add noodles and cook until soft, about 5 minutes. Remove from water and rinse in several changes of cold water until water is clear. Drain noodles and cut into 4-inch (10-cm) lengths to make them easier to eat.

To make noodle seasoning: In a bowl, combine noodle seasoning.

Add noodles to seasoning and mix well to coat. Add beef and mushrooms, spinach, carrots and onions and mix well. Serve sprinkled with pine nuts and ground sesame seeds, and topped with egg gidan.

Serves 4 or 5

Fried octopus with **chili pepper** sauce and **noodles**

Nakji bokkeum

Wash octopus to remove the salt. Cut body and tentacles into 2¹/₂-inch (6-cm) long pieces. Bring a medium-sized saucepan of salted water to the boil. Immerse octopus pieces in boiling water and remove just as it starts to curl, 2–3 minutes.

Bring a small saucepan of water to a boil. Cut mushrooms in half, then dip in boiling water for a few seconds. Remove and drain.

Cut scallions into 1¹/₂-inch (4-cm) lengths. Slice chili peppers lengthwise. Remove core and seeds and cut flesh into thin strips about 1¹/₂ inches (4 cm) long.

Peel onion and cut into bite-sized pieces.

To make sauce: Combine sauce ingredients in a medium-sized bowl and mix well.

Heat 1 tablespoon oil in a frying pan and stir-fry vegetables for about 2 minutes. Add octopus and sauce. Continue to stir-fry for 2–3 minutes, then remove from heat and cover to keep warm.

Meanwhile, bring 4 cups (32 fl oz/1 L) water to a boil. Add noodles and boil for 3 minutes. Remove from water, rinse thoroughly in cold water and drain.

Place hot octopus and cold noodles on a large plate for guests to serve themselves.

Serves 4

Ingredients

6¹/₂ oz (200 g) octopus or squid, cleaned and rubbed with salt

3 oz (90 g) fresh button mushrooms

6 medium scallions (shallots/spring onions)

3 fresh red chili peppers

1 small yellow (brown) onion

vegetable or sunflower oil for frying

5 oz (150 g) somyeon noodles (wheat-flour noodles)

FOR SAUCE

2 tablespoons red chili paste

2 tablespoons red chili powder

2 teaspoons light soy sauce

1 tablespoon crushed garlic

1 tablespoon finely chopped scallion (shallot/spring onion)

1 teaspoon sugar

pinch freshly ground black pepper

2 tablespoons sesame oil

1 tablespoon pan-toasted, ground sesame seeds

1 tablespoon vegetable or sunflower oil

Ingredients

5 oz (150 g) stewing (gravy) beef

½ teaspoon vegetable or sunflower oil for frying

10 cups (80 fl oz/2.5 L) water

1 tablespoon crushed garlic

1 packet (30) dumpling skins

1 egg, separated

salt and freshly ground black pepper to taste

2 daepa or scallions (shallots/spring onions), white parts only

FOR BEEF SEASONING

2 teaspoons light soy sauce

½ clove garlic, crushed

½ teaspoon sesame oil

kosher or sea salt, to taste

FOR DUMPLING FILLING

2 dried Chinese mushrooms, soaked for 30 minutes in several changes of water

12 oz (375 g) firm tofu

3 oz (90 g) Chinese cabbage kimchi

3 oz (90 g) ground (minced) beef

3 oz (90 g) bean sprouts, rinsed and trimmed

2 teaspoons kosher or sea salt

2 tablespoons finely chopped scallions (shallots/spring onions)

1 clove garlic, crushed

1 tablespoon pan-toasted, ground sesame seeds

½ tablespoon sesame oil

SOUPS

Dumpling soup
Manduguk

To make beef seasoning: In a glass or ceramic bowl, mix seasoning ingredients.

Slice beef into 1½-inch (4-cm) strips and mix with beef seasoning ingredients. Heat oil in a large saucepan and stir-fry beef over high heat until browned on all sides. Add water and garlic. Bring to a boil, reduce to a simmer and cook for 30 minutes. Leave beef in stock.

To make dumpling filling: Squeeze excess water from mushrooms. Remove and discard stems, and finely chop caps. Crush tofu and squeeze out water (place tofu on clean cotton towel, bring corners together, then twist bundle tightly). Finely chop kimchi and squeeze out liquid. Combine mushrooms, tofu, kimchi and beef in a large bowl. Mix in the remaining dumpling ingredients.

Place 1 tablespoon of dumpling filling in center of a dumpling skin. Wet outer edge of skin, then fold in half to make a half-moon shape, pressing edges together firmly. Repeat with remaining skins.

Fry egg white and yolk to make egg gidan (see step 9, page 42). Remove from pan and thinly slice.

Add dumplings to beef soup and simmer until dumplings rise to surface of stock, 3–4 minutes. Add salt and pepper to taste.

Slice daepa diagonally. Ladle soup into individual bowls, with 7 or 8 dumplings per bowl. Garnish with egg gidan and daepa and serve.

Serves 4

Ginseng chicken **soup**

Samgyetang

Spoon rice into cavity of chicken. Make a slit in flap of flesh on each side of cavity entrance. Push end of right drumstick through slit on left side and end of left drumstick through slit on right. Alternatively, tie or skewer cavity closed.

Place chicken in a large saucepan and cover with water. Add garlic, dates and ginseng. Bring to a boil, then reduce heat to low and simmer until liquid turns yellowish, about 1 hour.

Transfer whole chicken and liquid to a large bowl. Accompany with separate bowls of chopped scallion, salt and pepper for diners to add to taste.

Serves 1

Tip

It is believed that this hot soup is energy food. It is eaten in summer to energize the body by replacing lost body heat. The traditional wisdom is that hot food keeps the mind and body strong throughout the summer.

Right: Dumpling soup (Manduguk)

Ingredients

- ⅓ cup (1¾ oz/50 g) sticky (glutinous) rice, soaked in water for about 30 minutes
- 1 fresh young chicken (about 1¼ lb/500 g), washed
- 1 whole bulb garlic
- 5 dates
- 2 whole finger-thick, fresh ginseng roots, washed
- 1 scallion (shallot/spring onion), roughly chopped
- salt and freshly ground black pepper to taste

Ingredients

4 oz (125 g) stewing (gravy) beef

8 cups (64 fl oz/2 L) water

light soy sauce to taste

4 oz (125 g) ground (minced) beef

2 tablespoons all-purpose (plain) flour

2 eggs, beaten

vegetable or sunflower oil for frying

1 egg, separated

crown daisy leaves (ssukgat) for
  garnish (optional)

FOR STEWING BEEF SEASONING
1 teaspoon table salt

1 teaspoon sesame oil

1 teaspoon crushed garlic

freshly ground black pepper to taste

FOR GROUND BEEF SEASONING
1 teaspoon salt

2 teaspoons finely chopped scallions
  (shallots/spring onions)

1 oz (30 g) firm tofu, crumbled

1 teaspoon crushed garlic

1 teaspoon sesame oil

freshly ground black pepper to taste

Ingredients

12 oz (375 g) dried seaweed, soaked
  in cold water for 30 minutes

1 tablespoon sesame oil

1 tablespoon crushed garlic

6 oz (180 g) mussel meat (thin beef
  strips or clam meat can be
  substituted)

10 cups (80 fl oz/2.5 L) water

Korean soy sauce to taste

Beef ball soup
Wanjatang

To prepare and use stewing beef seasoning: Combine ingredients in a small bowl. Thinly slice beef and coat in seasoning. Transfer to a medium saucepan, add water and boil for 20 minutes. Add soy sauce to taste.

Meanwhile, mix ground beef in small bowl with ground beef seasoning ingredients. Using wet hands, form beef into bite-sized balls. Coat beef balls in flour and dip in the beaten egg.

Heat 1½ teaspoons of oil in a frying pan and stir-fry balls until evenly browned, about 2 minutes. Remove and drain on paper towels. Fry egg white and yolk to make egg gidan (see step 9, page 42). Remove from pan and slice into thin strips. Add beef balls to boiling beef stock. Reduce heat to low and simmer for 5 minutes. Serve beef balls and stock in individual bowls, garnish with egg gidan and crown daisy leaves.

Serves 4 or 5

Seaweed soup
Miyeokguk

Drain seaweed and cut into 4-inch (10-cm) lengths. Heat sesame oil in medium saucepan. Add garlic and mussels and stir-fry over high heat for 1 minute. Add seaweed and continue cooking for 2 minutes. Pour in water and bring to a boil. Reduce heat to low and simmer for 15–20 minutes. Ladle into individual bowls, add soy sauce to taste and serve.

Serves 4 or 5

Note: This soup is traditionally eaten at birthdays and by women after childbirth to assist in recovery.

Dumpling and rice cake **soup**
Tteok manduguk

Cover beef with water in a medium-sized saucepan. Bring to a boil, reduce to a simmer and cook for 30 minutes. Remove from water and thinly slice. Season with pepper, salt and sesame oil and set aside. Reserve beef stock for the soup.

To make dumpling filling: Squeeze excess water from kimchi, then finely chop. Bring a small saucepan of water to a boil. Immerse bean sprouts in boiling water for a few seconds. Remove, drain and chop roughly. Place kimchi, bean sprouts and pork in a medium-sized bowl. Mix in remaining filling ingredients.

Place 1½ tablespoons of filling in a skin. Wet outer edge of skin, then fold in two to make a half-moon shape, pressing the edges together firmly. (Note: Traditionally, after pressing dumplings into a half-moon shape, the opposite edges are pressed again to create a parcel shape.)

Transfer dumplings to a steamer and steam for 6–7 minutes over rapidly boiling water. Meanwhile, make egg gidan (see step 9, page 42) and cut into small diamond shapes.

Season beef stock to taste with Korean soy sauce, then bring to a boil. Once the stock is boiling, add the rice cakes and cook for 3 minutes. Add daepa, cooked beef and steamed dumplings, and return to a boil. Serve soup in large bowls, garnished with egg diamonds.

Serves 4 or 5

Tip
You can buy white (not yellow) dumpling wrappers from an Asian market.

Ingredients

7 oz (220 g) stewing (gravy) beef

freshly ground black pepper

table salt

sesame oil to taste

1 packet (30) dumpling skins

1 egg, separated to make egg gee-dan

4 oz (125 g) rice cakes

1 daepa or scallion (shallot/spring onion)

Korean soy sauce to taste

FOR DUMPLING FILLING
5 oz (150 g) Chinese (napa) cabbage kimchi

5 oz (150 g) bean sprouts, tops and tails trimmed

5 oz (150 g) ground (minced) pork

4 oz (125 g) tofu, drained and mashed

2 tablespoons finely chopped scallions (shallots/spring onions)

1 tablespoon crushed garlic

1 teaspoon ginger juice (obtained by grating fresh ginger)

1 teaspoon pan-toasted, ground sesame seeds

1 teaspoon table salt

1 teaspoon pepper

1 teaspoon sesame oil

Ingredients

1 long, thin zucchini (courgette)

4½ teaspoons table salt

1½ cups (12 fl oz/375 ml) water

3 dried Chinese mushrooms, soaked for 30 minutes in several changes of water

5 oz (150 g) ground (minced) beef

vegetable or sunflower oil for frying

1 egg, separated

1 tablespoon Korean soy sauce

1 tablespoon sugar

¼ cup (2 fl oz/60 ml) beef stock

pinch shredded red chili peppers

FOR BEEF AND MUSHROOM MARINADE

2 tablespoons light soy sauce

1 tablespoon sugar

4 teaspoons finely chopped scallions (shallots/spring onions)

2 teaspoons crushed garlic

2 teaspoons sesame oil

2 teaspoons pan-toasted, ground sesame seeds

freshly ground black pepper to taste

VEGETABLES

Stuffed zucchini
Hobakseon

Cut zucchini diagonally into pieces 1½ inches (4 cm) long. Make a lengthwise slit through each piece to within about ¼ inch (6 mm) of each end. Combine salt and water and soak zucchini pieces for about 30 minutes.

Meanwhile, squeeze excess water from mushrooms. Remove and discard stems, and finely chop caps.

To make beef and mushroom marinade: Combine beef and mushroom marinade ingredients in a glass or ceramic bowl.

Add ground beef and mushroom slices to marinade and set aside to marinate, 20–30 minutes.

Fry egg white and yolk to make egg gee-dan (see step 9, page 42). Remove from pan and slice into thin strips.

Heat 1 tablespoon oil in a frying pan and stir-fry the marinated beef and mushrooms over high heat for 2–3 minutes.

Remove zucchini from salted water. Gently squeeze out excess water, then drain on paper towels. Press beef and mushroom mixture into the slits in the zucchini.

Combine soy sauce, sugar and beef stock in a saucepan and bring to a boil. Add stuffed zucchini and boil for 1 minute. Reduce heat and simmer until zucchini is tender, spooning sauce over zucchini from time to time, 2–3 minutes.

Serve on a deep plate, garnished with egg gee-dan and shredded red chili pepper.

Serves 2

Three-color vegetables

Samsaek namul

Wash enoki mushrooms. Remove and discard stems. Bring 3 cups salted water to a boil. Immerse mushroom caps in boiling water for a few seconds. Remove and drain. Mix mushrooms in a medium bowl with salt, garlic, scallion, sesame seeds, sesame oil and pepper. Heat 1 teaspoon oil in a frying pan and fry mushroom mixture for 1–2 minutes. Remove from pan and keep warm.

Cut bell pepper in half lengthwise. Remove core and seeds. Cut flesh into thin strips. Heat 1 teaspoon oil in a frying pan. Add bell pepper strips and salt, and stir-fry for 1 minute. Add garlic, then scallion, sesame oil and sesame seeds. Stir-fry for 1 more minute. Remove from pan and keep warm.

If using fresh shiitake mushrooms, bring 3 cups salted water to a boil. Immerse mushrooms in boiling water for a few seconds. Remove, rinse in cold water and drain. Squeeze gently to remove excess water, then slice thinly. If using dried mushrooms, squeeze out excess water, remove and discard stems, and cut caps into thin slices.

In a medium bowl, mix mushroom slices, salt, garlic, scallion, sesame seeds, sesame oil and pepper. Heat 1 tablespoon vegetable oil in a frying pan and stir-fry mushroom mixture for 2–3 minutes. Remove from pan and keep warm.

Arrange 3 vegetables in separate piles on a white plate or in separate bowls, and serve with steamed rice.

Serves 4

Ingredients

FOR ENOKI MUSHROOMS
4 oz (125 g) fresh enoki (paeng-i) mushrooms

1½ teaspoons kosher or sea salt

1½ teaspoons crushed garlic

1 tablespoon finely chopped scallion (shallot/spring onion)

1 tablespoon pan-toasted, ground sesame seeds

1 tablespoon sesame oil

pinch of freshly ground black pepper

vegetable or sunflower oil for frying

FOR GREEN BELL PEPPER
1 green bell pepper (capsicum)

vegetable or sunflower oil for frying

1½ teaspoons kosher or sea salt

1½ teaspoons crushed garlic

1 tablespoon finely chopped scallion (shallot/spring onion)

1 tablespoon sesame oil

1 tablespoon pan-toasted, ground sesame seeds

FOR SHIITAKE MUSHROOMS
4 oz (125 g) fresh shiitake (ryogo) mushrooms or dried Chinese mushrooms, soaked for 30 minutes in several changes of water

1½ teaspoons kosher or sea salt

1½ teaspoons crushed garlic

1 tablespoon finely chopped scallion (shallot/spring onion)

1 tablespoon pan-toasted, ground sesame seeds

1 tablespoon sesame oil

pinch freshly ground black pepper

vegetable or sunflower oil for frying

Ingredients

SPINACH

pinch table salt

10 oz (300 g) spinach, roots removed, leaves and stems cut into 1½-inch (4-cm) lengths

1½ tablespoons Korean soy sauce

1 tablespoon finely chopped scallion (shallot/spring onion)

4½ teaspoons crushed garlic

1½ teaspoons sesame oil

1½ teaspoons pan-toasted, ground sesame seeds

CHINESE BELLFLOWER ROOT

vegetable or sunflower oil for frying

4 oz (125 g) prepared Chinese bellflower root

1 tablespoon sesame oil

1½ teaspoons table salt

1 tablespoon finely chopped scallion (shallot/spring onion)

1½ teaspoons crushed garlic

3 tablespoons water

4½ teaspoons sesame oil

4½ teaspoons pan-toasted, ground sesame seeds

shredded red chili peppers for garnish

Three-color vegetables

Fill a large saucepan with water, add salt and bring to a boil over high heat. Plunge spinach into water and boil, uncovered, until it is limp, 1–2 minutes. Remove and rinse in cold water, then drain. Gently squeeze out excess water.

In a small bowl, mix spinach, soy sauce, scallion, garlic and sesame oil. Sprinkle with ground sesame seeds; set aside.

Heat 1 tablespoon oil in a saucepan or frying pan with a lid. Add Chinese bellflower root and fry over medium heat for 2 minutes. Mix in 1 tablespoon sesame oil, salt, scallion, and garlic. Add water, cover and simmer until most of water has evaporated. Mix in sesame oil and sesame seeds. Remove from the heat and garnish with red chili peppers; set aside.

Remove firm section of fernbrake and cut remainder into 1½-inch (4-cm) lengths. Combine fernbrake marinade ingredients, add fernbrake and marinate for 20 minutes.

Heat 1 tablespoon oil in a frying pan and stir-fry fernbrake over high heat for 2–3 minutes. Add water, cover and simmer until most of water has evaporated, 3–4 minutes.

Remove from heat. Mix in sesame oil, sesame seeds and shredded chili pepper. Arrange the 3 vegetables on a plate and serve at room temperature with steamed rice.

Serves 4

FERNBRAKE
10 oz (300 g) prepared fernbrake

vegetable or sunflower oil for frying

¼ cup (2 fl oz/60 ml) water

1 tablespoon sesame oil

1 tablespoon pan-toasted, ground
   sesame seeds

pinch shredded red chili pepper

FOR FERNBRAKE MARINADE
2 tablespoons Korean soy sauce

1 teaspoon sugar

2 tablespoons chopped scallions
   (shallots/spring onions)

1 tablespoon crushed garlic

freshly ground black pepper to taste

Vegetables

Stuffed mushrooms with beef

Pyogojeon

Squeeze excess moisture from mushrooms. Remove and discard stems.

To make beef seasoning: Combine seasoning ingredients in a glass or ceramic bowl.

Add beef and tofu to beef seasoning and mix well. Lightly coat inside of each mushroom cap with flour, then fill with beef mixture, pressing in firmly.

To make dipping sauce: Mix dipping sauce ingredients together in a small bowl.

Dust filled mushrooms with flour, dip in beaten egg and fry in 1 tablespoon oil over high heat for about 2 minutes on stuffed side and 1 minute on second side (note: the egg prevents the stuffing from absorbing too much oil).

Serve mushrooms accompanied with dipping sauce and steamed rice.

Serves 4

Ingredients

12 dried Chinese mushrooms, soaked for 30 minutes in several changes of water

3 oz (90 g) beef tenderloin or scotch fillet

2 oz (60 g) tofu, drained and mashed with a fork

2 tablespoons all-purpose (plain) flour

1 egg, beaten

vegetable or sunflower oil for frying

FOR BEEF SEASONING

1 tablespoon light soy sauce

4½ teaspoons sugar

2 teaspoons finely chopped scallions (shallots/spring onions)

1 teaspoon crushed garlic

1 teaspoon sesame oil

1 teaspoon pan-toasted, ground sesame seeds

pinch freshly ground black pepper

FOR DIPPING SAUCE

2 tablespoons light soy sauce

1 tablespoon water

1 tablespoon white vinegar

1 tablespoon pan-toasted, ground pine nuts

Ingredients

7 oz (220 g) Chinese (napa) cabbage kimchi

½ medium yellow (brown) onion

5 oz (150 g) pork belly

vegetable or sunflower oil for frying

1 tablespoon crushed garlic

2 tablespoons finely chopped scallions (shallots/spring onions)

1 tablespoon sesame oil

1 tablespoon pan-toasted, ground sesame seeds.

1 block (16 oz/500 g) firm tofu

Kimchi and tofu
Dubu kimchi

Slice kimchi into pieces 1–1½ inches (2–4 cm) long. Peel onion and cut vertically into slices. Thinly slice pork belly. Heat 1 tablespoon oil in a frying pan. Add kimchi, onion, pork, garlic and scallions and stir-fry until pork is well cooked, 3–5 minutes. Turn off heat, add sesame oil and sesame seeds and mix in well.

Bring a medium-sized saucepan of water to a boil. Place tofu in water for a few seconds, then remove and drain. Cut tofu into pieces 1½ x ¾ inch (4 x 2 cm) in size and ½ inch (12 mm) thick. Place fried kimchi mixture in center of a serving plate, arrange tofu pieces around edge and serve with steamed rice.

Serves 4

Ingredients

1 medium squid tube (body), about 2–2½ oz (60–75 g), skinned and washed with water

3 oz (90 g) dried seaweed, soaked in water for about 15 minutes

1 small cucumber (preferably Joseon)

FOR SALAD DRESSING

1 scallion (shallot/spring onion)

2 tablespoons white vinegar

1 tablespoon water

1 teaspoon Korean soy sauce

½ teaspoon table salt

1 tablespoon water

½ lemon

Seaweed salad
Miyeokcho

Squeeze excess water from squid with a clean kitchen towel, then cut open and lay flat. Slice into bite-sized pieces, then score surface with tip of a sharp knife. Bring a medium-sized saucepan of salted water to a boil. Immerse seaweed in water for a few seconds. Remove, rinse in cold water and drain. Cut into strips about 1¼ inches (3 cm) long.

Cut cucumber in half lengthwise and then into slices about ½ inch (12 mm) thick. Roughly chop scallion and mix with salad dressing ingredients except lemon half. Cut lemon into thin slices and add to dressing. Combine all salad components in a large bowl, drizzle with dressing over and serve with steamed rice.

Serves 4

Beef and bamboo shoots

Juksunchae

Slice bamboo shoots diagonally into 1½-inch (4-cm) pieces. Bring rice water to a simmer in a large saucepan. Add bamboo shoots and dried chili pepper, and simmer uncovered for 1 hour. Remove bamboo shoots from water and set aside to cool. Peel and slice in half lengthwise. Heat 2 tablespoons oil in a frying pan and fry bamboo shoot slices over medium heat for 3–5 minutes. Repeat process for watercress stems, omitting dried chili.

Squeeze excess water from mushrooms. Remove and discard stems and cut caps into thin slices.

To make beef and mushroom marinade: Combine marinade ingredients in a large glass or ceramic bowl. Add beef and mushrooms and mix well to coat. Heat 1 tablespoon oil in a frying pan and stir-fry beef and mushrooms for 3–5 minutes.

Bring a small saucepan of salted water to a boil. Immerse bean sprouts in boiling water for a few seconds. Remove and drain.

Fry egg white and yolk to make egg gidan (see step 9, page 42). Reserve a few slices for garnish.

To make seasoning: Combine all ingredients in a large bowl.

Add all ingredients to seasoning, mix well to coat, then add chili strips. Transfer to a large platter, decorate with the reserved egg gidan and serve with steamed rice.

Serves 4

Ingredients

- 2 fresh bamboo shoots (about 10 oz/300 g each)
- 5 cups (40 fl oz/1.25 L) rice water (reserved after washing rice)
- 1 dried red chili pepper
- vegetable or sunflower oil for frying
- 2 oz (60 g) Korean watercress stems (minari)
- 3 dried Chinese mushrooms, soaked for 30 minutes in several changes of water
- 4 oz (125 g) beef tenderloin or scotch fillet, thinly sliced into strips about 1½ inches (4 cm) long
- 4 oz (125 g) bean sprouts, trimmed
- 1 egg, separated
- 1 medium red chili pepper, julienned into 1½-inch (4-cm) strips

FOR BEEF AND MUSHROOM MARINADE
- 2 tablespoons light soy sauce
- 1 tablespoon sugar
- 4 teaspoons finely chopped scallions (shallots/spring onions)
- 2 teaspoons crushed garlic
- 2 teaspoons sesame oil
- 2 teaspoons pan-toasted, ground sesame seeds
- freshly ground black pepper to taste

FOR SEASONING
- 2 teaspoons light soy sauce
- 2 teaspoons table salt
- 2 teaspoons sugar
- 1 tablespoon white vinegar
- 2 teaspoons pan-toasted, ground sesame seeds

Ingredients

- 1 sheet dried kelp, about 4 inches (10 cm) square
- 3 oz (90 g) dried anchovies (ikan bilis)
- 6 oz (180 g) firm tofu
- 1 daepa or scallion (shallot/ spring onion)
- 1 red chili pepper
- 1 green chili pepper
- 1 small zucchini (courgette)
- 4 tablespoons soybean paste
- 4 teaspoons hot red chili paste
- 1 oz (30 g) stewing (gravy) beef, sliced thinly into 1½-inch (4-cm) strips
- 1 tablespoon crushed garlic

Tofu and vegetable soup
Toenjangguk

Bring 2 cups (16 fl oz/500 ml) water to a boil in a medium saucepan. Add kelp and anchovies, and boil for 15–20 minutes to make a stock.

Meanwhile, cut tofu into pieces ½ inch (1 cm) thick. Slice daepa, and red and green chili peppers diagonally into pieces ¹⁄₁₆ inch (2 mm) thick. Cut zucchini in half lengthwise, then into half-moon slices.

Add soybean paste and red chili paste to stock and stir to dissolve. Add beef and garlic to stock, then tofu, daepa and zucchini. Reduce heat to medium and cook for about 5 minutes, then add chili peppers.

Ladle into individual bowls and serve hot with steamed rice.

Serves 4

Ingredients

5 oz (150 g) large mussels, meat only

2 oz (60 g) beef tenderloin or scotch fillet

1 clove garlic

1 knob fresh ginger (same size as a garlic clove)

1 scallion (shallot/spring onion), white part only

2 tablespoons light soy sauce

1 cup (8 fl oz/250 ml) water

1 tablespoon sugar

1 tablespoon freshly ground black pepper

1 tablespoon sesame oil

1 tablespoon cornstarch (cornflour), mixed with 1 tablespoon water

1 tablespoon pine nuts, pan-toasted and ground

SEAFOOD

Mussels with soy dressing
Honghapcho

Bring a large pot of salted water to a boil. Place mussels in the boiling water and boil for 2 minutes. Remove from water and drain.

Slice beef into thin strips about 1¼ inches (3 cm) long.

To make dressing, slice garlic, ginger and scallion into strips 1¼ inches (3 cm) long. Place in a medium saucepan and add soy sauce, water, sugar, pepper and sesame oil. Add beef to dressing. Bring to a boil and cook for 5 minutes. Add mussels and cornstarch-water mixture. Reduce heat to low and simmer for 5 minutes longer, spooning liquid over mussels from time to time.

Arrange mussels on a serving plate, sprinkle with the pine nuts and serve with steamed rice.

Serves 4

Variation
While not traditional, if you wish to retain the mussel shells, use 16 oz (500 g) mussels in this recipe. When boiling mussels in salted water (as above), boil for 2 minutes, then discard any shells that do not open.

Mussel **kabobs**

Bring a large saucepan of salted water to a boil. Add mussel meat, cover and cook for about 2 minutes. Remove mussels from water and drain.

To make seasoning sauce: Combine seasoning sauce ingredients in a large saucepan. Bring to a boil, stirring to dissolve sugar.

Add mussels and garlic to saucepan, reduce heat to low and simmer until mussels become shiny, about 10 minutes. Sprinkle with sesame oil and stir carefully to coat. Remove mussels from sauce.

Thread mussels and bell pepper strips alternately onto skewers—use 4 mussels per skewer. End each with a garlic clove.

Heat kabobs in a little oil in a very hot frying pan or on an oiled grill just before serving. Place a kabob on each plate and sprinkle with ground pine nut powder to serve.

Serves 4

Ingredients

meat from 16 large mussels

4 cloves garlic, peeled

1 teaspoon sesame oil

1 medium green bell pepper (capsicum), cut into strips about 1½–2 inch (4–5 cm)

vegetable or sunflower oil for frying

4 bamboo skewers, 5 inches (13 cm) long, soaked in water for 30 minutes

1 tablespoon pan-toasted, ground pine nuts

FOR SEASONING SAUCE

2 tablespoons light soy sauce

1 tablespoon sugar

1 tablespoon ginger juice (obtained by grating fresh ginger)

2 tablespoons water

1 teaspoon rice wine

pinch table salt

Squid kabobs

Using the tip of a knife, score surface of squid in a crisscross pattern to prevent it over-curling. Bring a large saucepan of water to a boil. Add squid and cook until it just starts to curl, about 3 minutes. Drain and slice squid into strips $\frac{3}{4}$ inch (2 cm) wide and $2\frac{1}{2}$ inches (6 cm) long.

Remove cores and seeds from bell peppers and cut into pieces roughly the same size as squid strips.

Combine chili paste, sugar, garlic, scallions, ginger juice, sesame seeds, sesame oil and liquid wheat gluten in a medium bowl and mix well. Thread strips of squid and bell pepper alternately onto skewers. Brush each kabob with chili paste mixture, coating both sides of squid and bell peppers.

Cook kabobs for 1 minute on each side in 1 teaspoon of oil in a very hot frying pan or on an oiled grill, being careful not to burn them. Place one kabob on each plate and serve with steamed rice.

Serves 4

Ingredients

- 3 medium squid tubes (bodies), about 6½ oz (200 g) total, cut open and cleaned
- 4 small green bell peppers (capsicums)
- 5 tablespoons red chili paste
- 2 tablespoons sugar
- 2 tablespoons crushed garlic
- 3 scallions (shallots/spring onions), finely chopped
- 1 teaspoon ginger juice (obtained by grating fresh ginger)
- 1 teaspoon pan-toasted, ground sesame seeds
- 1 teaspoon sesame oil
- 1 tablespoon liquid wheat gluten
- vegetable or sunflower oil for frying
- 15 bamboo skewers 5 inches (13 cm) long, soaked in water for 30 minutes

Ingredients

3 medium squid tubes (bodies), about 6½ oz (200 g) total, cut open and cleaned

4 fresh shiitake mushrooms or dried Chinese mushrooms soaked for 30 minutes in several changes of water

2 small green bell peppers (capsicums), cut into bite-sized pieces

2 tablespoons vegetable or sunflower oil

lettuce leaves for serving

1 teaspoon pan-toasted sesame seeds

1 teaspoon freshly ground black pepper

1 teaspoon thin hot red chili pepper strips

FOR MARINADE

3 tablespoons light soy sauce

2 tablespoons sugar

2 tablespoons crushed garlic

2 scallions (shallots/spring onions), finely chopped

1 teaspoon ginger juice (obtained by grating fresh ginger)

1 teaspoon sesame oil

Squid bulgogi
Ojing-eo bulgogi

Using the tip of a knife, score surface of squid in a crisscross pattern to prevent it over-curling during cooking. Cut squid into bite-sized pieces.

If using fresh shiitake mushrooms, dip in rapidly boiling water for a few seconds. Remove and drain on paper towels, then chop roughly. If using dried mushrooms, squeeze out excess water. Remove and discard stems and roughly chop caps.

To make marinade: Combine marinade ingredients in a small bowl and mix well.

Place squid, mushrooms and bell peppers in a large glass or ceramic bowl with marinade and marinate for 20–30 minutes.

Heat oil in a frying pan or on a grill until very hot. Drain squid, mushroom and green pepper pieces and cook over high heat until liquid has evaporated and marinade has caramelized, about 5 minutes.

Arrange lettuce leaves on individual plates and place squid bulgogi in center. Sprinkle with sesame seeds, black pepper and chili pepper strips, and serve with steamed rice.

Serves 4

Ingredients

3 medium squid tubes, about 6½ oz (200 g) total, cut open and cleaned

2 medium cucumbers

lettuce leaves for serving

1 tablespoon pan-toasted sesame seeds

FOR SOUR RED CHILI PASTE SAUCE

5 tablespoons red chili paste

3 tablespoons sugar or liquid wheat gluten

3 tablespoons white vinegar

1 teaspoon ginger juice (obtained by grating fresh ginger)

Squid with sour red **chili paste** sauce

Using the tip of a knife, score the inside surface of squid body in a crisscross pattern to prevent it over-curling during cooking.

Bring a large saucepan of water to a boil. Add squid to the water and boil until it just starts to curl, about 3 minutes. Drain and cut into pieces 1½ inches (4 cm) long and ⅜ inch (1 cm) wide.

Cut cucumber in half lengthwise, then slice diagonally into 2-inch (5-cm) lengths. Bring a medium saucepan of water to a boil. Immerse cucumber pieces in boiling water for a few seconds. Remove, rinse in cold water and drain.

To make red chili paste sauce: Combine sauce ingredients in a large bowl.

Add squid and cucumber to chili paste sauce, and mix well to coat.

Arrange lettuce leaves on a serving plate and place squid and cucumber in the center. Sprinkle with sesame seeds and serve with steamed rice.

Serves 4

Steamed **dried pollack** fish

Bugeojjim

Pound dried fish with a meat mallet or rolling pin to tenderize flesh. Soak in cold water for about 1 hour. Remove from water and drain. Spread fish out flat on a board, belly side down. Cut off tail and fins. Press down firmly on spine along entire length of fish. Turn fish and remove spine by taking hold of one end and peeling it away. Use pliers to remove any other bones. Cut flesh into bite-sized pieces.

To make steaming sauce: Combine sauce ingredients in a medium-sized bowl.

Dip pieces of fish one by one in sauce, coating them well. Transfer to a medium-sized saucepan and add any remaining sauce. Cover and cook over medium heat until fish is tender, about 30 minutes.

Fry egg white and yolk separately to make egg gee-dan (see step 9, page 42). Remove from pan and slice into thin strips.

When fish is tender, add scallions, chili pepper, egg gee-dan and ground pine nuts. Cook over medium heat for 3–5 minutes longer to heat through. Transfer to a deep plate and serve with steamed rice.

Serves 4

Ingredients

- 2 pieces dried pollack or dried cod, each 3½ oz (100 g)

- 1 egg, separated

- 2 scallions (shallots/spring onions), cut diagonally into 1½-inch (4-cm) lengths

- 1 small dried red chili pepper

- 1 tablespoon pan-toasted, ground pine nuts

FOR STEAMING SAUCE

- ¼ cup (2 fl oz/60 ml) light soy sauce

- 2 tablespoons sugar

- 3 tablespoons finely chopped scallions (shallots/spring onions)

- 4½ teaspoons crushed garlic

- 2 teaspoons crushed fresh ginger

- 4½ teaspoons pan-toasted, ground sesame seeds

- 4½ teaspoons sesame oil

- freshly ground black pepper to taste

- 2 cups (16 fl oz/500 ml) water

Octopus **kabobs**
Nakji sanjeok

Clean octopus by removing eyes, mouth area, viscera and ink sac (or have your seafood supplier do this for you). Wash octopus, rub thoroughly with salt, then wash again in clean water.

Bring a large saucepan of water to a boil. Immerse octopus in boiling water until it starts to curl, about 3 minutes. Drain and cut body and tentacles into strips about $3/4$ inch (12 mm) wide and $2^1/2$ inches (6 cm) long.

Bring a medium-sized saucepan of water to a boil. Wipe oyster mushrooms clean, then immerse in boiling water for a few seconds. Remove and drain.

Remove core and seeds from bell peppers, then cut into pieces about same size as pieces of octopus.

Thread octopus, mushrooms and bell peppers alternately onto skewers.

To make chili paste sauce: Combine ingredients in a small bowl.

Brush kabobs well with chili paste sauce mixture.

Cook kabobs for about 1 minute on each side in 2 tablespoons oil in a very hot frying pan or on an oiled grill, taking care not to burn them. Arrange kabobs on a plate and serve with steamed rice.

Serves 4

Ingredients

1 medium octopus, about 1 lb (500 g)

kosher or sea salt

7 oz (220 g) oyster mushrooms

4 green bell peppers (capsicums)

20 bamboo skewers, 5 inch (13 cm) long, soaked in water for 30 minutes

2 tablespoons vegetable or sunflower oil

FOR RED CHILI PASTE SAUCE

5 tablespoons red chili paste

2 tablespoons sugar

1 tablespoon liquid wheat gluten

2 tablespoons crushed garlic

3 tablespoons finely chopped scallions (shallots/spring onions)

1 teaspoon ginger juice

1 tablespoon pan-toasted, ground sesame seeds

1 tablespoon sesame oil

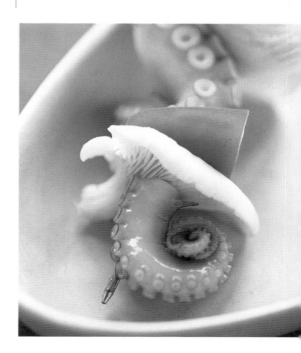

Ingredients

8 large fresh shrimp (prawns),
  shells and heads intact

7 oz (220 g) stewing (gravy) beef

1 medium cucumber

table salt

4 oz (125 g) cooked bamboo shoots

white pepper

vegetable or sunflower oil for frying

FOR PINE NUT SAUCE

6 tablespoons pan-toasted, ground
  pine nuts

1/4 cup (2 fl oz/60 ml) beef stock

1 teaspoon table salt

1 teaspoon sesame oil

pinch white pepper

Steamed shrimp with **pine nut** sauce

Wash shrimp. Leaving shells and heads intact, carefully cut down backbone to expose and remove vein. Steam shrimp until they turn red, 7–8 minutes. Allow to cool, then peel off shells and remove heads. Slice flesh diagonally into pieces about 1$\frac{1}{4}$ inches (3 cm) long and set aside.

Place beef in a medium saucepan, cover with water and bring to a boil. Cook for 30 minutes, then remove from water and wrap in a clean kitchen towel. Place a heavy weight, such as a large can in a frying pan, on beef and allow to cool and firm, about 20 minutes. When cool, cut into $\frac{1}{16}$-inch (2-mm) thick slices.

Cut cucumber in half lengthwise, then cut diagonally into thick slices. Sprinkle slices with salt, leave to sweat for 5–10 minutes, then squeeze out excess water.

Cut bamboo shoots in half lengthwise, then cut diagonally into $\frac{1}{16}$-inch (2-mm) thick slices. Sprinkle with a little salt and white pepper. Heat a little oil in a frying pan and fry slices for 1–2 minutes, then drain and cool on paper towels.

To make pine nut sauce: Combine sauce ingredients in a bowl.

Place shrimp, beef, cucumber and bamboo shoots in a large serving bowl. Sprinkle with salt and white pepper. Pour pine nut sauce over top, toss lightly to coat and serve with steamed rice.

Serves 4

Grilled fish

Saengseon gui

Clean and rinse the fish, leaving fins and head attached. Using the tip of a knife, cut slits on both sides of flesh every $\frac{1}{2}$ inch (12 mm) or so to allow the marinade to penetrate.

Combine sesame oil and soy sauce, then coat fish with the mixture.

To make marinade: Combine marinade ingredients in a small bowl and mix well.

Heat 3 tablespoons oil in a frying pan or grill pan until very hot. Place fish in pan and cook until half done, about 10 minutes. Turn over and cook other side until half cooked, about 10 minutes. Reduce heat to medium, coat fish with the marinade and cook until marinade darkens, about 10 minutes. Turn over and repeat.

Transfer fish to an oval plate and serve.

Variation
Use the soy sauce marinade instead of the red chili pepper marinade.

Ingredients

- 2 flounder or sole, about 10 oz (300 g) each
- 1 tablespoon sesame oil
- 1 tablespoon soy sauce
- vegetable or sunflower oil

FOR RED CHILI MARINADE
- 2 tablespoons red chili paste
- 2 tablespoons finely chopped scallions (shallots/spring onions)
- 1 tablespoon crushed garlic
- 4$\frac{1}{2}$ teaspoons crushed ginger
- 1 tablespoon sesame oil
- 1 tablespoon pan-toasted, ground sesame seeds
- pinch black or white pepper

SOY SAUCE MARINADE
- $\frac{1}{3}$ cup (3 fl oz/90 ml) light soy sauce
- 1 tablespoon sugar
- 1 tablespoon crushed garlic
- 2 tablespoons finely chopped scallions (shallots/spring onions)
- 1$\frac{1}{2}$ teaspoons crushed ginger
- 1$\frac{1}{2}$ teaspoons pan-toasted, ground sesame seeds
- 1$\frac{1}{2}$ teaspoons sesame oil
- freshly ground black pepper

Ingredients

4 oz (125 g) radish (mu)

¾ oz (20 g) crown daisy leaves or roughly chopped celery

1 scallion (shallot/spring onion)

1 oz (30 g) Korean watercress stems

1 green chili pepper

1 red chili pepper

2 oz (60 g) enoki (paeng-i) mushrooms

2 oz (60 g) clams or pipis, cleaned

3 oz (90 g) mussel meat without shell

4 medium shrimp (prawns), deveined

1 medium crab, cleaned and cut into quarters

1 medium octopus

4 littleneck clams (or pipis), cleaned

1 tablespoon table salt

3½ oz (105 g) udon noodles

FOR STOCK

¾ oz (20 g) dried anchovies

4-inch (10-cm) square of dried kelp

6 cups (48 fl oz/1.5 L) water

FOR SEASONING

3 tablespoons red chili powder

1 tablespoon crushed garlic

2 teaspoons table salt

1 tablespoon finely chopped scallion (shallot/spring onion)

½ teaspoon freshly ground black pepper

½ teaspoon ginger juice (obtained by grating fresh ginger)

2 tablespoons rice wine

Mixed seafood casserole

Haemul jeon-gol

To prepare stock: Cook anchovies and kelp in water for 30 minutes over medium heat. Set stock aside.

Slice radish into 1-inch (2.5-cm) squares. Cut crown daisy, scallion and watercress stems into 2-inch (5-cm) lengths. Slice green and red chili peppers diagonally, then remove cores and seeds.

Cut root from enoki mushrooms and separate individual mushrooms.

To prepare seasoning: In a small bowl combine all seasoning ingredients, then add to the stock.

Place radish in the bottom of a saucepan. Arrange clams, mussels, mushrooms, shrimp, crab, octopus, and littleneck clams in layers on top of radish, sprinkle with salt and then cover with stock.

Cook on high heat, bring to a boil and cook for 15 minutes. Add crown daisy leaves, watercress stems, scallion, chili peppers, and mushrooms and cook on high heat for 5 minutes. Add udon noodles and cook for 2 minutes. Place saucepan in the center of table with individual bowls for guests to help themselves.

Serves 4

CHICKEN

Seasoned **whole chicken**

Dakjjim

To prepare seasoning: In a medium bowl combine all seasoning ingredients. Set aside to allow the flavors to blend.

Meanwhile, place chicken in a large pot and cover with water. Bring to a boil, skimming off any froth from the surface. Pour in half of seasoning mixture and continue boiling for 15 minutes longer. Add potato, carrot, onions, daepa and remaining seasoning mixture. Continue boiling until vegetables are tender but not mushy, 15–20 minutes. Test chicken by inserting a skewer in a piece of breast meat. Chicken is cooked when juices run clear. Remove from heat. Reserve liquid.

Fry egg white and yolk in oil to make egg gee-dan (see step 9, page 42). Remove from pan and slice into thin strips.

Place segments of chicken in serving bowls, garnish with small amounts of reserved liquid, garnish with egg gee-dan and serve.

Serves 4

Ingredients

4-lb (2-kg) whole chicken, washed, dried and chopped into 2-inch (5-cm) pieces

1 large potato, peeled and cut into 1-inch (2.5-cm) cubes

1 large carrot, peeled and cut into 1-inch (2.5-cm) cubes

3 medium yellow (brown) onions, peeled, each cut into 8 wedges

½ lengthwise daepa or scallion (shallot/spring onion), cut into 1-inch (2.5-cm) lengths

1 egg, separated

1 tablespoon vegetable or sunflower oil for frying

FOR SEASONING

¾ cup (6 fl oz/180 ml) light soy sauce

¼ cup (2 oz/60 g) sugar

3 tablespoons finely chopped scallions (shallots/spring onions)

3 tablespoons crushed garlic

2 tablespoons ginger juice (obtained by grating fresh ginger)

3 tablespoons rice wine

1 teaspoon sesame salt

pinch freshly ground black pepper

sesame oil to taste

Ingredients

6 chicken wings, wing tips removed

pinch sesame salt

1 tablespoon ginger juice (obtained by grating fresh ginger)

¼ cup (1 oz/30 g) cornstarch (cornflour)

1½ cups vegetable or sunflower oil for frying

sesame oil to taste

FOR SWEET SAUCE

2 tablespoons light soy sauce

1 tablespoon malt liquid (mullyeot)

1 tablespoon sugar

1 teaspoon ginger juice (obtained by grating fresh ginger)

1 tablespoon rice wine

3 tablespoons water

5 whole cloves garlic

2 red chili peppers, halved lengthwise, seeds removed

2 green chili peppers, halved lengthwise, seeds removed

Sweet chicken wings
Dangnalgae gangjeong

Wash chicken wings and pat dry with paper towels.

Combine sesame salt and ginger juice in a bowl, then add chicken wings. Mix well to coat in juice. Remove wings and coat with cornstarch.

Heat oil in a wok or deep frying pan until very hot. Fry wings until golden, about 10 minutes. Remove from oil and drain on paper towels.

To make sweet sauce: Combine soy sauce, malt liquid, sugar, ginger juice, rice wine and water in a medium saucepan and bring to a boil. Add garlic and red and green chili peppers and stir in well. Continue boiling the sauce until reduced by half.

Add chicken wings to saucepan and mix to coat with sauce. Transfer chicken wings, garlic and chili peppers to a serving plate, sprinkle with sesame oil and serve with steamed rice.

Serves 4

Fried chicken breast

Dakgaseum gui

Wash chicken breast and pat dry on paper towels. Cut into bite-sized pieces, then score with tip of knife to allow seasoning to penetrate.

In a glass or ceramic bowl, mix soy sauce, sugar, rice wine, ginger juice, garlic, daepa, sesame salt, pepper and sesame oil. Add chicken and mix well to coat. Cover and refrigerate to marinate for 2–3 hours. The longer chicken marinates, the more intense the flavor and more tender the meat will be.

Heat 2 tablespoons oil in a frying pan until very hot. Add chicken pieces and stir-fry until golden, 3–5 minutes. Remove from pan and drain on paper towels.

Arrange lettuce leaves on a serving plate, top with chicken pieces and serve with steamed rice.

Serves 4

Hint
If you like your chicken spicy, replace the soy sauce with 3 tablespoons of red chili paste and salt to taste.

Ingredients

10 oz (300 g) boneless chicken breast

3 tablespoons light soy sauce

2 tablespoons sugar

2 tablespoons rice wine

1 teaspoon ginger juice (obtained by grating fresh ginger)

1 tablespoon crushed garlic

1 daepa or scallion (shallot/spring onion), finely chopped

1 teaspoon sesame salt

pinch freshly ground black pepper

sesame oil to taste

vegetable or sunflower oil for frying

lettuce leaves for serving

Ingredients

5 chicken drumsticks

1 tablespoon ginger juice (obtained by grating fresh ginger)

1 tablespoon vegetable or sunflower oil

2 tablespoons light soy sauce

1 tablespoon sugar

1 tablespoon malt liquid (mullyeot)

1 tablespoon rice wine

1 tablespoon chopped parsley for garnish

Grilled chicken drumsticks
Dakdari gui

Score drumsticks all over with tip of a knife to allow ginger flavor to penetrate. Place drumsticks in a medium bowl and drizzle with ginger juice. Marinate for 15 minutes, turning frequently to coat with juice.

Heat 1 tablespoon of oil in a frying pan over medium heat. Add drumsticks and fry until golden, about 5 minutes. Remove and keep warm. Keep sauce in pan.

Add soy sauce, sugar, malt liquid and rice wine to pan juices. Boil over high heat until liquid is reduced by half, about 5 minutes.

Using a brush, coat drumsticks with the sauce. Return to frying pan and cook over high heat until sauce caramelizes and chicken is cooked, 5–8 minutes. Test with a skewer; chicken is done when juices run clear.

Transfer drumsticks to a serving plate and wrap the bone ends in foil. Garnish with parsley and serve as finger food with steamed rice.

Serves 4

Chicken kabobs
Daksanjeok

Wash chicken breast fillets and pat dry with paper towels. Place each fillet between sheets of plastic wrap and pound to about ¼ inch (6 mm) thick with a meat mallet. Cut edges of fillets with a knife tip every 2 inches (5 cm) or so to prevent fillet from curling and shrinking when cooked. Sprinkle with salt and pepper.

Heat 1 tablespoon oil in a frying pan until very hot but not smoking. Add chicken fillets and fry for about 2 minutes on each side. Remove from pan and set aside.

To make seasoned soy sauce: Boil soy sauce, sugar, malt liquid, ginger juice, rice wine and water in a saucepan until thick.

Add chicken to saucepan and simmer for 10–15 minutes. Remove chicken from saucepan, add sesame oil and allow to cool. Slice chicken into strips 1½ inches (4 cm) long.

Fry egg white and yolk to make egg gee-dan (see step 9, page 42). Remove from pan and slice into thin strips. Heat ½ teaspoon oil in a frying pan and fry daepa for about 30 seconds.

Thread chicken strips and daepa pieces alternately onto skewers. Leave about 1½ inches (4 cm) free at one end for holding the skewer.

To serve, arrange skewers on an oval plate and garnish with egg gee-dan and chili pepper strips.

Serves 4

Ingredients

3 lb (1.5 kg) chicken breast fillets

salt and freshly ground black pepper

vegetable or sunflower oil for frying

sesame oil to taste

1 egg, separated

1 daepa or scallion (shallot/spring onion), cut into 1½-inch (4-cm) pieces

4 bamboo skewers 5 inches (13 cm) long, soaked in water for 30 minutes

½ fresh red chili pepper, seeds removed, cut into thin strips

FOR SEASONED SOY SAUCE
5 tablespoons light soy sauce

2 tablespoons sugar

1 tablespoon malt liquid (mullyeot)

1 tablespoon ginger juice (obtained by grating fresh ginger)

1 tablespoon rice wine

¼ cup (2 fl oz/60 ml) water

Ingredients

10 oz (300 g) pork tenderloin, cut into pieces 1½ inches (4 cm) wide by 2 inches (5 cm) long

¼ cup (1 oz/30 g) cornstarch (cornflour)

2 cups (16 fl oz/500 ml) vegetable or sunflower oil for deep-frying

3 cloves garlic, peeled and finely sliced

1 fresh red chili pepper, seeds removed, cut into 1¼-inch (3-cm) strips

3 daepa or scallions (shallots/spring onions), cut into 2-inch (5-cm) lengths

2 tablespoons light soy sauce

2 tablespoons malt liquid (mullyeot)

freshly ground black pepper

sesame oil to taste

lettuce leaves for serving

FOR MARINADE
4½ teaspoons table salt

1 tablespoon ginger juice (obtained by grating fresh ginger)

2 tablespoons rice wine

Fried pork with green onions
Jeyuk bokkeum

To make marinade: Combine marinade ingredients in a medium-sized glass or ceramic bowl.

Add pork pieces, cover and refrigerate to marinate for 2–3 hours. Remove pork pieces from marinade and coat with cornstarch. Heat oil in a wok or deep frying pan over high heat. Add pork cubes one at a time so they do not stick together and fry for 1 minute. Remove from oil and drain on paper towels.

Heat 1 tablespoon oil in a wok or frying pan over medium heat and stir-fry garlic and chili pepper for 2 minutes. Add pork and continue stir-frying for 3–5 minutes. Add daepa, soy sauce, malt liquid and pepper and stir-fry for 1 minute. Sprinkle with sesame oil. Arrange lettuce leaves on a large plate, spoon fried pork and daepa into center and serve.

Serves 4

Barbecued **beef**

Bulgogi

1. Cut beef into ¼-inch (0.5-cm) thick slices then into thin strips (see note below). Score surface with the tip of a knife to allow marinade flavors to penetrate. Grate pear to provide 1 tablespoon of pear juice.

2. Marinate beef in pear juice and rice wine in a glass or ceramic bowl for 30 minutes. Combine soy sauce, sugar, scallion, garlic, ground sesame seeds, sesame oil and pepper in large bowl. Mix in beef, cover and refrigerate to marinate for 2–3 hours.

3. Cut yellow onion, green pepper and carrot into bite-sized pieces and set aside.

4. Remove beef slices from marinade and broil or grill to the preferred tenderness. Arrange beef on lettuce leaves and serve hot, accompanied by pieces of raw vegetable.

Serves 2

Tip
For added bite, accompany vegetables with a dipping sauce of red chili paste and soybean paste.

Note: Traditionally, beef bulgogi is made with wide, thin shavings of beef. But as this is the most common beef cut available in Western markets, we have adjusted the recipe.

Ingredients

7 oz (220 g) beef tenderloin or scotch fillet

1 pear (preferably nashi), peeled

1½ teaspoons rice wine

4½ teaspoons light soy sauce

1 tablespoon sugar

1 tablespoon finely chopped scallion (shallot/spring onion)

1½ teaspoons crushed garlic

1 tablespoon pan-toasted, ground sesame seeds

1½ teaspoons sesame oil

freshly ground black pepper to taste

1 medium yellow (brown) onion, peeled

1 green bell pepper (capsicum), core and seeds removed

1 small carrot, peeled

2 lettuce leaves for serving

1

2

3

4

Ingredients

10 oz (300 g) pork tenderloin

vegetable or sunflower oil for grilling

FOR MARINADE

½ medium yellow (brown) onion, peeled and finely chopped

2 tablespoons red chili paste

2 tablespoons light soy sauce

2 tablespoons finely chopped scallions (shallots/spring onions)

1 tablespoon crushed garlic

1½ teaspoons grated fresh ginger

1 tablespoon sesame oil

1 tablespoon pan-toasted, ground sesame seeds

freshly ground black pepper to taste

Grilled pork
Jeyuk gui

Cut pork into strips about ¼ inch (6 mm) thick and 1½ inches (4 cm) long. Score surface with the tip of a knife to allow marinade to penetrate.

To make marinade: Combine all marinade ingredients in a glass or ceramic bowl.

Dip pork strips into marinade piece by piece to ensure they are well coated, add to marinade, cover and refrigerate to marinate for 2–3 hours.

If you have a portable grill plate, brush it with oil and set in center of serving table. Grill pork strips in front of your guests and serve immediately. Otherwise, broil (grill) pork in a broiler (grill) or in a lightly oiled grill pan or frying pan. Serve with steamed rice.

Serves 4

Boiled beef
Pyeonyuk

Ingredients

26 oz (815 g) stewing (gravy) beef

10 cups (80 fl oz/2.5 L) water

5 cloves garlic, peeled and crushed

8 fresh black peppercorns

1 daepa or scallion (shallot/
spring onion)

1/4 cup (2 fl oz/60 ml) light soy sauce

FOR SOUR SOY SAUCE

5 tablespoons light soy sauce

2 tablespoons finely chopped
scallions (shallots/spring onions)

1 teaspoon crushed garlic

2 tablespoons sugar

1 tablespoon pan-toasted, ground
sesame seeds

2 tablespoons white vinegar

1 1/2 teaspoons red chili powder

1/2 teaspoon freshly ground black
pepper

Soak beef in cold water for 30 minutes to clean. Transfer beef to a large saucepan, add water, garlic, peppercorns, daepa and soy sauce. Bring to a boil and cook for 30–40 minutes. Test with a skewer. If the juices run clear, the meat is cooked.

Remove beef from saucepan and wrap in a clean kitchen towel. Place a heavy weight, such as a large can in a frying pan, on beef and leave to cool and flatten for about 2 hours. Thinly slice the beef and set aside.

Remove daepa from saucepan and slice white portion into pieces about 1 1/2 inches (4 cm) long (discard green portion). Cut pieces lengthwise into thin strips, place in a bowl of cold water for a few seconds, then drain.

To make sour soy sauce: Combine sauce ingredients in a bowl and mix well.

Arrange beef pieces on a plate, sprinkle with daepa strips, and serve accompanied by sour soy sauce.

Serves 4

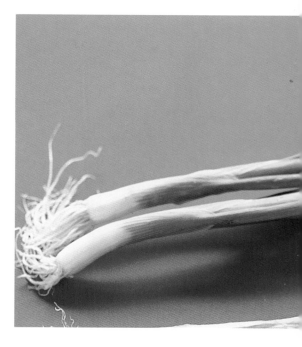

Ingredients

7 oz (220 g) beef tenderloin or scotch fillet

1 oz (30 g) jjokpa or scallions (shallots/spring onions)

1 green bell pepper (capsicum)

4 skewers, 5 inches (12 cm) long, soaked in water for 30 minutes

vegetable or sunflower oil for frying

lettuce leaves for serving

FOR MARINADE

2 tablespoons light soy sauce

2 teaspoons sugar

1 scallion (shallot/spring onion), finely chopped

1 teaspoon pan-toasted, ground sesame seeds to a powder

1 teaspoon sesame oil

Beef kabobs
Sogogi sanjeok

Cut beef into strips about $^3/_4$ inch (2 cm) wide by $^1/_4$ inch (6 mm) thick by $2^1/_2$ inches (6 cm) long. Score surface with the tip of a sharp knife.

To make marinade: Combine all marinade ingredients in a medium glass or ceramic bowl.

Mix beef strips in marinade and marinate for 15–20 minutes.

Cut jjokpa into strips 2 inches (5 cm) long. Remove core and seeds from bell pepper and cut into slices 2 inches (5 cm) long.

Thread alternate pieces of beef, jjokpa and bell pepper alternately onto each skewer, leaving about $1^1/_4$ inches (3 cm) free for holding skewer.

Heat 1 tablespoon oil in a frying pan over a high heat. Fry kabobs for 2 minutes on each side. Arrange lettuce leaves on a serving plate, place kabobs in center and serve.

Serves 4

Beef with **pine nut** sauce

Sogogi jatjeup pyeonuk chae

Cover beef with water in a large saucepan. Bring to a boil and cook until tender, about 30 minutes. Remove from water and wrap in a clean cotton or linen cloth on a work surface. Place a heavy weight, such as a large can in a frying pan, on beef and leave to cool and firm for about 2 hours. Remove from cloth and cut into slices ¹/₂ inch (1 cm) thick and 2 inches (4 cm) long.

Trim celery stalk and slice diagonally into ¹/₂-inch (12-mm) pieces. Slice cucumber in half lengthwise and cut into slices ¹/₂ inch (12 mm) thick and 2 inches (5 cm) long. Peel pear and cut it into similar-sized pieces. Sprinkle with sugar to prevent it from turning brown.

Cut radish in half lengthwise, then into half-moon slices ¹/₄ inch (6 mm) thick.

To make pine nut sauce: Place pine nuts, milk and salt in a blender and process to a paste.

Place beef, celery, cucumber, pear, radish, vinegar, salt, and mustard in a large bowl. Spoon in pine nut paste and mix well to coat. Decorate a serving plate with celery leaves, place bowl of beef in center and serve cold.

Serves 4

Ingredients

7 oz (220 g) stewing (gravy) beef

1 celery stalk

1 small cucumber

¹/₂ pear (preferably nashi)

2 teaspoons sugar

1 red radish

2 teaspoons white vinegar

1 teaspoon table salt

¹/₂ teaspoon hot mustard

celery leaves for garnish

FOR PINE NUT SAUCE
¹/₃ cup (2 oz/60 g) pine nuts

2 tablespoons milk

pinch table salt or to taste

Ingredients

½ cup (4 fl oz/125 ml) pear juice or ½ cup (4 oz/125 g) grated pear (preferably nashi)

3 tablespoons rice wine

2 lb (1 kg) beef tenderloin or scotch fillet

1 daepa or scallion (shallot/spring onion)

1 fresh red chili pepper

shiso leaves or lettuce leaves for serving

FOR MARINADE

2 tablespoons table salt

3 tablespoons sugar

3 tablespoons finely chopped scallions (shallots/spring onions)

2 tablespoons crushed garlic

1 tablespoon pan-toasted, ground sesame seeds

freshly ground black pepper to taste

3 tablespoons sesame oil

Salt **bulgogi**

Combine pear juice and rice wine in a medium glass or ceramic bowl. Slice beef into strips ¼ inch (6 mm) thick. Add to bowl and marinate for 30 minutes.

To make marinade: Combine marinade ingredients in a large glass or ceramic bowl.

Drain beef, add to marinade and mix well. Cover and refrigerate to marinate for 2–3 hours.

Cut daepa into 1½-inch (4-cm) sections, then slice lengthwise into very thin strips. Place in a bowl of cold water for a few seconds, then drain. Slice chili pepper in half lengthwise, remove seeds and membrane and slice into thin strips. Heat broiler (grill). Remove beef strips from marinade and broil (grill) to the desired tenderness.

Arrange shiso leaves on a plate. Place beef on leaves, sprinkle with daepa and chili pepper strips, and serve with steamed rice.

Serves 4

Hint

As Salt bulgogi does not have any sauce, drizzle with a little sesame oil to give it a sheen.

Steamed beef spare ribs

Galbijjim

Cut beef spare ribs into 2-inch (5-cm) sections. Place in a large bowl of water and soak for 1 hour to clean.

Place ribs in a large saucepan, add water and bring to a boil. Boil until liquid reduces by half, 15–20 minutes.

To make marinade: Combine marinade ingredients in a medium glass or ceramic bowl.

Remove ribs from beef stock. Add in two-thirds of marinade to beef stock, and cook over medium heat for about 20 minutes.

Peel daikon and carrot and cut into bite-sized cubes. Immerse cubes in rapidly boiling water for about 1 minute, then remove and set aside. Squeeze excess water from the mushrooms. Remove and discard stems. Leave caps whole.

Add remaining marinade, daikon and carrot, and beef ribs to stock. Continue cooking until ribs are very tender, about 20 minutes.

Fry egg white and yolk to make egg gee-dan (see step 9, page 42). Remove from pan and cut into diamond shapes 1/2 inch (12 mm) long.

Arrange spare ribs on a serving dish, garnish with egg diamonds and serve with steamed rice.

Serves 4

Ingredients

20 oz (600 g) beef spare ribs

4 cups (32 fl oz/1 L) water

1/2 medium daikon or 10 peeled chestnuts

1 medium carrot

8 dried Chinese mushrooms, soaked for 30 minutes in several changes of water

1 egg, separated

FOR MARINADE
6 tablespoons light soy sauce

6 tablespoons pear juice or grated pear

3 tablespoons sugar

2 scallions (shallots/spring onions), finely chopped

2 cloves garlic, crushed

1 tablespoon sesame oil

1 tablespoon pan-toasted, ground sesame seeds

2 tablespoons malt liquid (mullyeot)

freshly ground black pepper to taste

Ingredients

5 oz (150 g) firm tofu

10 oz (300 g) ground (minced) beef
2 tablespoons light soy sauce

1 teaspoon table salt

1 tablespoon sugar

2 tablespoons finely chopped
   scallions (shallots/spring onions)

1 tablespoon crushed garlic

1 tablespoon pan-toasted, ground
   sesame seeds

1 tablespoon sesame oil

vegetable or sunflower oil for frying

2 teaspoons pan-toasted, ground pine
   nuts

Ingredients

14 oz (425 g) minced (ground) beef

2 tablespoons crushed garlic

1 teaspoon black pepper

1 tablespoon sesame oil

vegetable or sunflower oil for frying

1 teaspoon sesame oil

4 fresh gingko nuts

20 pine nuts

1 teaspoon malt liquid (mullyeot)

4 skewers, 5 inches (13 cm) long,
   soaked in water for 30 minutes

FOR SAUCE
2 tablespoons light soy sauce

2 teaspoons sugar

2 teaspoons rice wine

3 tablespoons water

Seobsanjeok

Wrap tofu in a clean kitchen towel and squeeze out water. Transfer tofu to a bowl and mash with a fork. Add beef, soy sauce, salt, sugar, scallions, sesame seeds, and sesame oil and combine until mixture becomes sticky.

Form beef mixture into 2 patties and place on a sheet of oiled aluminum foil. Heat broiler (grill) and cook patties to desired doneness, 5–7 minutes on each side. Remove from grill and set aside until cool enough to handle. Slice each patty into $1^{1}/_2$-inch x $^{3}/_4$-inch (3-cm x 2-cm) pieces, arrange on a plate, sprinkle with ground pine nuts and serve.

Serves 4

Seobsanjeok kabobs

Using your hands, mix beef with garlic, pepper and sesame oil until mixture becomes sticky. Divide mixture into 4 pieces and shape into patties. Place patties on a sheet of oiled aluminum. Heat a broiler (grill) or frying pan and cook patties for 2–3 minutes on each side.

To prepare and use sauce: Combine ingredients in a medium saucepan, bring to a boil and cook, stirring, for 2–3 minutes. Add patties, reduce heat to medium and cook until browned, 10–15 minutes. Turn off heat and stir in sesame oil.

Add 1 teaspoon oil to a frying pan over medium heat and fry gingko nuts until they become transparent. Remove from heat and rub between sheets of paper towel to remove skins. Slice surface of pine nuts the tip of a knife, then brush with malt liquid. Insert a skewer horizontally through each beef patty, then through 1 gingko nut. Stud each patty with 5 pine nuts and serve.

Serves 4

Honey **dates**
Daechucho

Wipe dates with damp kitchen towel, then use a small knife to remove pits. If dates are too dry, place in a bowl, sprinkle with rice wine and leave for 3 hours to swell.

Place 2 or 3 pine nuts inside each date, making sure some protrude through opening. Drizzle a little honey over the filled dates. Transfer dates to a medium-sized saucepan. Add remaining honey and cook over low heat, stirring to mix dates and honey. The dates are cooked when they turn black. Separate dates and arrange on a serving dish, pine nut side up.

Serves 4

Ingredients

20 small fresh or dried dates

1/2 cup (4 fl oz/125 ml) rice wine

2 tablespoons pine nuts

3 tablespoons honey

Sticky rice pancakes Hwajeon

Place salt, water and sticky rice powder in a large bowl. Mix together to form a dough. Transfer dough to a floured surface. Roll out to about 1 inch (2.5 cm) thick. Using a cookie cutter or drinking glass, cut out pancakes 2 inches (5 cm) in diameter.

Remove pits from dates and cut dates into thin slices. Separate crown daisy leaves. Heat 1/2 teaspoon oil in a frying pan or on a grill plate. Fry each pancake on one side, pressing down with the back of a spoon, until transparent. Turn and decorate with sliced dates and daisy leaves. Continue cooking for 1 minute longer. Remove from pan, brush with honey and serve (hot pancakes will make brushing honey easy).

Makes 20 pancakes

Ingredients

1 teaspoon table salt

1/2 cup (4 fl oz/125 ml) hot water

4 cups (13 oz/400 g) sticky rice powder

4 dates

2/3 oz (20 g) crown daisy leaves

4 tablespoons vegetable or sunflower oil

1/2 cup (4 fl oz/125 ml) honey

Ingredients

5 cups (25 oz/780 g) powdered malt

48 cups (384 fl oz/12 L) water

5 cups (25 oz/780 g) sticky (glutinous) rice

1 small knob ginger, about ⅓ oz (10 g)

4 cups (2 lb/1 kg) sugar

¼ cup (2 oz/60 g) pine nuts

Ingredients

½ cup (4 oz) Maximowiczia chinenesis (omija) berries (available from Korean food stores and from sellers of Chinese medicines)

5 cups (40 fl oz/1.25 L) water

1 cup (8 oz/250 g) sugar

½ medium nashi or other firm pear

1 teaspoon pine nuts

Rice and malt drink
Sikhye

Soak malt in water for about 3 hours. After soaking, use your hands to rub malt pieces between your palms to break them down to small crystals. Strain soaked malt liquid through a fine-mesh sieve into a large bowl. Allow malt to settle, pour off clear liquid, and discard malt. Cook rice in a rice cooker (or steam for about 30 minutes).

Transfer cooked rice and malt liquid to a large saucepan. Leave in a warm place until rice rises to surface, 3–4 hours. Skim rice from surface of liquid. Wash in 2–3 changes of cold water, then drain. Peel ginger and thinly slice. Add ginger slices and sugar to malt liquid. Bring to a boil and cook for 20–30 minutes. Strain, discard ginger slices and set aside to cool. Ladle cooled liquid into glass dessert bowls. Add 1–2 tablespoons of rice, garnish with pine nuts, and serve.

Makes 30–40 drinks

Berry punch
Omijacha

Wash berries, then immerse them in 2 cups of water and leave to soak overnight. Strain through a very fine strainer, retaining the water (discard berries). In a small saucepan, mix remaining water with sugar and bring to a boil, stirring to dissolve sugar. Remove from heat and allow to cool. Combine cooled sugar syrup with strained omija water.

Peel pear and cut into decorative shapes using a vegetable cutter. Immerse pear shapes in syrup. Serve Omijacha in a glass dessert bowl, garnished with pear shapes and pine nuts. Add a pinch of salt if it tastes too sour.

Makes about 4 drinks

Nashi pear dessert
Baesuk

Ingredients

- 2 oz (60 g) peeled and sliced fresh ginger
- 10 cups (80 fl oz/2.5 L) water
- 1 large nashi (bae) or other firm pear
- 1 teaspoon black peppercorns
- 1½ cups (12 oz/275 g) sugar
- 1 tablespoon pine nuts

Boil ginger in water until water darkens in color, about 15 minutes. Remove from heat, strain water into a large saucepan and discard ginger. Peel pear and cut it into 6–8 segments or half moon shapes. Stud edges of each with peppercorns, pressing them in firmly so they do not fall out during cooking. Immerse pear segments in the ginger water and sugar, and simmer until soft, about 10 minutes. Remove from water and set aside to cool. Ladle 1 cup (8 fl oz/250 ml) ginger water into individual bowls. Add a slice of pear, garnish with 2 or 3 pine nuts and serve.

Serves 6–8

Cinnamon cookies
Maejakgwa

Ingredients

- 1 cup (5 oz/150 g) all-purpose (plain) flour
- ½ teaspoon table salt
- ⅔ oz (20 g) fresh ginger
- 3 tablespoons water
- 3 cups (24 fl oz/750 ml) vegetable or sunflower oil
- 2 tablespoons pan-toasted, ground pine nuts

FOR HONEY AND CINNAMON SYRUP
- 1 cup (8 fl oz/250 ml) water
- 1 cup (8 oz/250 g) sugar
- 2 tablespoons honey
- ½ teaspoon ground cinnamon

Sift flour and salt together into a bowl. Peel and finely grate ginger. Knead grated ginger, flour and water together to make a dough. Wrap dough in a damp kitchen towel and allow to rest for about 30 minutes.

To make honey and cinnamon syrup: Bring water and sugar to a boil without stirring. Continue boiling until reduced by half. Remove from heat and allow to cool, then add honey and cinnamon, and stir well.

Roll out dough on a floured work surface until about ¼ inch (6 mm) thick. Cut into rectangles about 1 inch x 2½ inches (2.5 cm x 6 cm). Heat oil until it reaches 300°F (150°C) on a deep-frying thermometer and deep-fry cookies until they turn light brown, 2–3 minutes. Remove from oil and drain on paper towels. Dip cookies in honey and cinnamon syrup, drain off excess and serve sprinkled with ground pine nut.

Makes 30 biscuits

Ingredients

2 oz (60 g) fresh ginger

6 cups (48 fl oz/1.5 L) water

1 oz (30 g) whole cinnamon

1½ cups (12 oz/375 g) sugar

4 small dried seedless persimmons or 2 medium dried seedless persimmons, halved

pine nuts for garnish

Cinnamon fruit punch with dried persimmon
Sujeonggwa

Peel ginger and thinly slice. Put sliced ginger, water and cinnamon in a large saucepan. Bring to a boil, then lower heat and simmer for 30–40 minutes. Add sugar and combine well, then strain through a fine-mesh sieve; discard ginger and cinnamon.

Remove stems from persimmon and add persimmons to cinnamon and ginger water 3 hours before serving to allow them to soften.

Ladle persimmons into glass bowls and fill with cinnamon and ginger water. Garnish with 2 or 3 pine nuts and serve.

Serves 4

Ingredients

3 cups (16 oz/500 g) soybeans

1 cup (6 oz/185 g) barley

14 cups (112 fl oz/3.5 L) water

4 lb (2 kg) fermented soybean powder

4 cups (2 lb/1 kg) kosher or sea salt

1 cup (5 oz/150 g) dried red chili pepper seeds (optional)

½ cup (4 fl oz/125 ml) malt liquid (mullyeot)

Soybean **paste**
Doenjang

Soak soybeans in water overnight, uncovered, at room temperature. Place soybeans in a saucepans with 6 cups (40 fl oz/1.5 L) water, cover and bring to a boil. Turn down heat to low and simmer until soybeans are soft enough to mash, 6–8 hours. Soak barley in 4 cups (32 fl oz/1 L) of the water for 30 minutes. Transfer to a large saucepan, more cups of water and simmer until a porridge forms, 6–8 hours, stirring occasionally.

Combine soybean powder, 4 cups (32 fl oz/1 L) of water and 3 cups of the salt in a large bowl. Mix thoroughly with soybeans and barley, then add chili pepper seeds, again mixing thoroughly. Transfer to a clay pot or glass container and sprinkle with remaining cup of salt over. Leave in a cool place for 7–10 days to allow salt to penetrate soybeans. Spread malt liquid on top. Cover pot with close-weave cloth, then lid. Leave in a cool place for 20–30 days to mature before use. Do not store in refrigerator. Soybean paste will keep for up to 1 year.

Makes 20 cups (160 fl oz/5 L)

Hint

If you do not wish to prepare your own soybean paste, it is readily available from Korean markets.

Hot **red chili** paste

Gochujang

Ingredients

10 lb (5 kg) malt liquid (mullyeot)

7½ cups (52 fl oz/1.9 L) water

1 lb (500 g) kosher or sea salt

1 packet fine soybean powder, about 15 oz (450 g)

2 lb 6 oz (1.28 kg) red chili powder

Boil malt and water together over high heat. Add salt and return to a boil. Turn off heat and allow to cool. Mix in fermented soybean powder and red chili powder until no lumps remain.

Store mixture in a clay pot or glass container, covered with a close-weave cloth. Leave pot outside in the sun for 1–2 weeks before bringing inside for use. The paste is ready in 20–30 days. Uncover pot only when it's a s.   ny while storing. It will keep for up to 1 year.

Makes 20   ′160 fl oz/5 L)

Hint

If you do not wish to prepare your own hot red chili paste, it is readily available from Korean and Asian markets.

Ingredients

6 tablespoons Korean soy sauce

2 scallions (shallots/spring onions), finely chopped

1½ (12 fl oz/375 ml) cups water

2 tablespoons pan-toasted, ground sesame seeds

¼ cup (2 oz/60 g) sugar

2 tablespoons crushed garlic

2 tablespoons sesame oil

¼ teaspoon freshly ground black pepper

2 medium yellow (brown) onions, peeled and grated

Beef marinade

Bulgogi yangnyeom

Combine all the ingredients in a large glass or ceramic bowl. Add sliced beef and mix well to coat. Cover and refrigerate to marinate for 2–3 hours. This amount of marinade is sufficient for 20 oz (600 g) of beef.

Tip

You can use rice wine or pear juice instead of the water. It makes the beef tender.

Glossary

Beef

Many recipes call for stewing (gravy) beef. May also be known as boneless beef chuck or chuck steak.

Cucumber

Korean recipes usually call for small pickling cucumbers, though small (English hothouse) cucumbers may be substituted. The smaller varieties tend to have fewer seeds and less water.

Dongchimi kimchi

This is a watery kimchi made from Korean round radish. Available from Korean markets.

Fermented anchovies

Made from salted fresh anchovies. Alternate layers of anchovies and salt are placed in a ceramic pot until it is full. A final thick layer of salt goes on top, then the pot is sealed and left in a cool place for 2–3 months to ferment.

Fernbrake or fiddlehead fern

The young shoots of the ferns are parboiled and dried. The dried ferns are soaked in water before use. Do not use wild ferns in recipes, as they may have absorbed harmful substances from the soil.

Green onions: Daepa and Jiokpa

The thick green onions, "daepa," are immature onions with a long, green top section and a shorter, white stem (about $1/2$ inch/12 mm in diameter) rising from an undeveloped bulb. "Jiokpa," the thin green onions, have a milder taste than the more mature green onions. They can be used interchangeably.

Lentil jelly

Purchase in rectangular blocks. In winter, store lentil jelly in a cool place for 1–2 days only. In summer, refrigerate lentil jelly for only 1 day as it will become dry. The jelly also comes in powder form. Mix powder with water to form the jelly.

Malt liquid

Malt liquid has a slightly sweet flavor. It is added to dishes for presentation as it adds a shine.

Maximowiczia chinensis (Omija) berries

"Omija," referring to the five tastes (sour, bitter, pungent, sweet, and salty) is used in Chinese medicine and as the basis for teas and liquors. Believed to stimulate the activity of the internal organs and to reduce fatigue, the drink made of these berries is a popular thirst-quencher.

Medium-grain rice

The small white grains of this oval rice are the most popular variety in the Korean diet.

Mushrooms

Shiitake mushrooms are used dried or fresh. If dried, they should be soaked before use for 30 minutes in several changes of water. The stems are then removed and discarded. Enoki mushrooms (paeng-i mushrooms) come in small, white clumps of thin stalks topped by tiny mushroom caps. They are mild in flavor and have a slight crunch.

Mustard greens (mustard leaves)

Dark green and peppery, these leaves are a prime source of vitamins A and C, thiamin and riboflavin. They are available fresh or frozen year-round in supermarkets and Asian markets.

Nashi pears

These yellowish-brown or green pears are the preferred choice of Korean cooks. Similar in appearance to an apple, they are crisp and juicy.

Noodles

"Dangmyeon" are sweet potato starch noodles used in Japchae (see page 48). Potato or mung bean noodles are light and slippery, buckwheat noodles are usually served cold (substitute Japanese soba noodles), udon noodles are soft, thick wheat noodles, and somyeon are thin, dried wheat noodles used in Hot noodles (see recipe page 45).

Persimmons (Gam)

This large, bright orange fruit is picked unripe, then peeled and hung out to dry until a white mold forms. The fruit is then used in punch (see recipe page 118).

Pine nuts

These high-fat nuts are mainly used in Korean recipes pan-toasted and ground, then sprinkled on finished dish as a garnish. If the strong pine flavor of the Chinese variety is too strong, purchase the Mediterranean variety used in making pesto.

Pollack

This small variety of cod is usually bought dried. The roe is popular preserved with salt and ground chili pepper. Substitute with pine nuts.

Radish: Japanese Daikon and Korean round

Similar to the daikon, but more difficult to obtain in the West, is the Korean round radish. The peppery taste of the giant white radish makes it popular in Korean and Japanese main and side dishes.

Red beans

The same beans as appear in chili con carne, red beans are used in Korea at the time of the winter solstice ("dongji," the day the sun comes to life again) to make red-bean porridge. The beans are also believed to combat illness and to drive away evil spirits.

Rice wine (Mukgeol-li)

Korean rice wine is a low-alcohol beverage with a slightly golden color, somewhat like that of olive oil. It is often used to add a slight sweetness.

Sesame oil

This nutty-tasting, dark oil made from toasted, crushed sesame seeds is used in Korean dishes for its taste and for the gloss it gives to the ingredients. It will last for up to a year at room temperature and almost indefinitely in the refrigerator.

Sesame salt

A combination of white sesame seeds and table salt. This ingredient can be made in large quantities and stored for later use. To make, heat seeds over low heat in an unoiled frying pan until golden and puffed up. Shake the pan during cooking to ensure the seeds cook evenly. When seeds are light brown, mix in salt, then remove from pan. When cool, grind seeds to a powder. Store in an airtight container until required.

Sesame seeds

Nutty in flavor and rich in oil, these seeds come in black, white and golden varieties. Pan-toasted and ground, the white seeds are popular as a garnish for Korean dishes.

Shiso/perilla leaves (Kkaennip)

These aromatic leaves are available from Japanese and Korean markets. They are sold fresh in small plastic packages and are used in a variety of ways: as a garnish, fried or as a tasty addition in sushi rolls.

Soybean paste (Doenjang)

Made from fermented soybean cakes, chili pepper and salt, this paste, also known as miso, is one of the most popular foods in Korea because it is said to contain cancer-fighting elements. High in protein, "doenjang" is also believed to be effective in lowering cholesterol levels. It is used in soups, stews, sauces and dips.

Sticky rice powder

Made from ground sticky (glutinous) rice, the powder is used as a spongy dough for sweet dumplings, cakes, pastries and wrappers.

Index

A

Abalone porridge 38

B

Baechu kimchi 22

Baek kimchi 29

Baesuk 117

Bamboo shoots, beef and 69

Barbecued beef 99

Beef

    ball soup 54

    and bamboo shoots 69

    barbecued 99

    boiled 101

    kabobs 102

    marinade for 121

    with pine nut sauce 105

    salt bulgogi 105

    seobsanjeok 110

    seobsanjeok kabobs 110

    steamed spare ribs 109

    stuffed mushrooms with 65

Bell pepper, three-color

    vegetables 61

Berry punch 114

Bibimbap

    about 8

    fresh vegetable 40

    recipe for 42

Bibimmyeon 46

Boiled beef 101

Bugeojjim 79

Bulgogi

    about 8

    barbecued beef 99

    salt 105

    squid 76

Bulgogi yangnyeom 121

C

Chicken

    breast, fried 91

    ginseng chicken 53

    kabobs 95

    seasoned whole 89

Chicken drumsticks, grilled 92

Chicken wings, sweet 90

Chili peppers

    about 17

    hot red paste 121

    sour red chili paste sauce

    with squid 78

Chinese bellflower root

    about 17

    three-color vegetables 62

Chinese cabbage

    about 17

    kimchi 25

    white kimchi 29

Cinnamon cookies 117

Cinnamon fruit punch with dried

    persimmon 118

Cold noodles 47

Cookies, cinnamon 117

Crown daisy leaves, about 18

Cucumber, stuffed 26

D

Daechucho 113

Dakdari gui 92

Dakgaseum gui 91

Dakjjim 89

Daksanjeok 95

Dangnalgae gangjeong 90

Dates, honey 113

Doenjang 120

Dried persimmon with cinnamon

    fruit punch 118

Dried pollack fish, steamed 79

Drinks

    berry punch 114

    cinnamon fruit punch with

    dried persimmon 118

rice and malt 114

Dubu kimchi 66

Dumplings

    and rice cake soup 57

    soup 52

F

Fermented shrimp, about 18

Fernbrake (fiddlehead fern)

    about 18

    three-color vegetables 62

Fish

    grilled 85

    steamed dried pollack 79

Fresh vegetable bibimbap 40

Fried chicken breast 91

Fried octopus with chili pepper

    sauce and noodles 51

Fried pork with green onions 96

Fruit punch, cinnamon, with

    dried persimmon 118

G

Galbijjim 109

Gimchi see Kimchi

Ginger, about 18

Ginko nuts, about 18

Ginseng root

    about 18

    chicken soup 53

Glutinous rice see Sticky rice

Gochujang 121

Green lentil jelly 32

Green onions

    about 19

    with fried pork 96

Grilled chicken drumsticks 92

Grilled fish 85

Grilled pork 100

Gujeolpan

    about 8

    recipe for 34

H

Haemul jeon-gol

    about 8

    recipe for 86

Haepari naengchae 33

Hobakseon 58

Honey dates 113

Honghapcho 72

Hot noodles 45

Hot red chilli paste 121

Hwajeon 113

J

Japchae

    about 8

    recipe for 48

Jatjuk 37

Jellyfish strips

    about 19

    with vegetables 33

Jeonbokjuk 38

Jeyuk bokkeum 96

Jeyuk gui 100

Juksunchae 69

K

Kabobs

    beef 102

    chicken 95

    mussel 72

    octopus 81

    seobsanjeok 110

    squid 75

Kimchi

    about 10

    Chinese cabbage 25

    and tofu 66

    watery radish 22

    white chinese cabbage 29

Kongjuk 38

L

Lentil jelly

    about 19

    green 32

M

Maejakgwa 117

Malt liquid

    about 19

    and rice drink 114

Manduguk 52

Marinade for beef 121

Mixed seafood casserole 86

Miyeokcho 66

Miyeokguk 54

Mung beans

    about 17

    pancakes 31

    porridge 37

Mushrooms

    about 20

    stuffed with beef 65

    three-color vegetables 61

Mussels

    kabobs 72

    with soy dressing 72

N

Naengmyeon

    about 8

    recipe for 47

Nakji bokkeum 51

Nakji sanjeok 81

Napa cabbage see Chinese

    cabbage

Nashi pear dessert 117

Nokdu bindaetteok 31

Nokdujuk 37

Noodles

    about 20

    cold 47

    with fried octopus and chili

    pepper sauce 51

    hot 45

O

Octopus

    fried, with red chili pepper

    sauce and noodles 51

    kabobs 81

Oi sobaegi 26

Ojing-eo bulgogi 76

Omijacha 114

P

Pancakes

    Korean mung bean 31

    sticky rice 113

Patjuk 39

Perilla leaves (shiso leaves),

    about 21

Persimmon, dried, with

    cinnamon fruit punch 118

Pine nuts

    porridge 37

    sauce, with beef 105

    sauce, with steamed shrimp

    82

Pollack fish, steamed dried 79

Pork

    fried, with green onios 96

    grilled 100

Porridge

    abalone 38

    mung bean 37

    pine nut 37

    read bean 39

soybean 38

Punch

    berry 114

    cinnamon fruit, with dried

    persimmon 118

Pyeonyuk 101

Pyogojeon 65

R

Radish

    about 20

    kimchi 22

Red bean porridge 39

Rice cakes

    about 20

    and dumpling soup 57

Rice, sticky see Sticky rice

S

Saengseon gui 85

Salad, seaweed 66

Salt

    about 19

    bulgogi 105

Samgyetang 53

Samsaek namul 61

Sanchae bibimbap 40

Seafood casserole 86

Seasoned whole chicken 89

Seaweed

    about 20, 21

    salad 66

soup 54

Seobsanjeok 110

   kabobs 110

Shisi leaves, about 21

Shrimp

   fermented, about 18

   steamed, with pine nut sauce 82

Sikhye 114

Sogogi jatjeup pyeonyuk chae 105

Sogogi sanjeok 102

Soup

   beef ball 54

   dumpling 52

   dumpling and rice cake 57

   ginseng chicken 53

   seaweed 54

   tofu and vegetable 70

Sour red chili paste sauce with

   squid 78

Soy sauce, about 21

Soybeans

   about 17

   paste 120

   porridge 38

Spare ribs, steamed beef 109

Spinach, three-color vegetables

   62

Squid

   bulgogi 76

   kabobs 75

   with sour red chili paste

sauce 78

Steamed beef spare ribs 109

Steamed dried pollack fish 79

Steamed shrimp with pine nut

   sauce 82

Sticky rice

   about 21

   and malt drink 114

   pancakes 113

Stuffed cucumber 26

Stuffed mushrooms with beef 65

Stuffed zucchini 58

Sujeonggwa 118

Sweet chicken wings 90

T

Tangpyeongchae 32

Three-color vegetables 61, 62

Toenjangguk 70

Tofu

   about 21

   kimchi and 66

   and vegetable soup 70

Tteok manduguk 57

V

Vegetables

   bibimbap 40

   with jellyfish 33

   three-color 61

   and tofu soup 70

W

Wanjatang 54

Watercress, about 19

Watery radish kimchi 22

White chinese cabbage kimchi 29

Z

Zucchini, stuffed 58

Guide to weights and measures

The conversions given in the recipes in this book are approximate. Whichever system you use, remember to follow it consistently, thereby ensuring that the proportions are consistent throughout a recipe.

WEIGHTS

Imperial	Metric
1/3 oz	10 g
1/2 oz	15 g
3/4 oz	20 g
1 oz	30 g
2 oz	60 g
3 oz	90 g
4 oz (1/4 lb)	125 g
5 oz (1/3 lb)	150 g
6 oz	180 g
7 oz	220 g
8 oz (1/2 lb)	250 g
9 oz	280 g
10 oz	300 g
11 oz	330 g
12 oz (3/4 lb)	375 g
16 oz (1 lb)	500 g
2 lb	1 kg
3 lb	1.5 kg
4 lb	2 kg

VOLUME

Imperial	Metric	Cup
1 fl oz	30 ml	
2 fl oz	60 ml	1/4
3 fl oz	90 ml	1/3
4 fl oz	125 ml	1/2
5 fl oz	150 ml	2/3
6 fl oz	180 ml	3/4
8 fl oz	250 ml	1
10 fl oz	300 ml	1 1/4
12 fl oz	375 ml	1 1/2
13 fl oz	400 ml	1 2/3
14 fl oz	440 ml	1 3/4
16 fl oz	500 ml	2
24 fl oz	750 ml	3
32 fl oz	1L	4

USEFUL CONVERSIONS

1/4 teaspoon	1.25 ml
1/2 teaspoon	2.5 ml
1 teaspoon	5 ml
1 Australian tablespoon	20 ml (4 teaspoons)
1 UK/US tablespoon	15 ml (3 teaspoons)

Butter/Shortening

1 tablespoon	1/2 oz	15 g
1 1/2 tablespoons	3/4 oz	20 g
2 tablespoons	1 oz	30 g
3 tablespoons	1 1/2 oz	45 g

OVEN TEMPERATURE GUIDE

The Celsius (°C) and Fahrenheit (°F) temperatures in this chart apply to most electric ovens. Decrease by 25°F or 10°C for a gas oven or refer to the manufacturer's temperature guide. For temperatures below 325°F (160°C), do not decrease the given temperature.

Oven description	°C	°F	Gas Mark
Cool	110	225	1/4
	130	250	1/2
Very slow	140	275	1
	150	300	2
Slow	170	325	3
Moderate	180	350	4
	190	375	5
Moderately Hot	200	400	6
Fairly Hot	220	425	7
Hot	230	450	8
Very Hot	240	475	9
Extremely Hot	250	500	10